W9-CIK-136

Catherine Wagner
From *American Classroom*
Emerson College Classroom, 1985

What you do not know is the only thing you know

T.S. Eliot. *Four Quartets. East Coker*, III. 1940.

SPITWAD SUTRAS

Classroom Teaching as Sublime Vocation

ROBERT INCHAUSTI

BERGIN & GARVEY
Westport, Connecticut • London

Library of Congress Cataloging–in–Publication Data

Inchausti, Robert.
    Spitwad sutras : classroom teaching as sublime vocation / Robert
Inchausti.
        p.   cm.
    Includes bibliographical references and index.
    ISBN 0–89789–365– 4 (alk. paper).—ISBN 0–89789–379– 4 (pbk. alk.
paper)
    1. Teachers—United States. 2. Teaching. 3. Classroom
management—United States. I. Title.
LB1775.2.I53   1993
371.1′02—dc20   93–25017

British Library Cataloguing in Publication Data is available.

Library of Congress Catalog Card Number: 93–25017
ISBN: 0–89789–365– 4 (HB)
ISBN: 0–89789–379– 4 (PB)

First published in 1993

Bergin & Garvey, 88 Post Road West, Westport, CT 06881
An imprint of Greenwood Publishing Group, Inc.

Printed in the United States of America

The paper used in this book complies with the
Permanent Paper Standard issued by the National
Information Standards Organization (Z39.48–1984).

10 9 8 7 6 5 4 3 2 1

This book is dedicated to all beginning teachers—may you find your true calling. And written in gratitude to my parents, Eva and Michael Inchausti; to my wife, Linda Garcia; and to my children, Monica and Nicholas, for reminding me to seek mine.

What the teacher "teaches" is by no means chiefly in the words he speaks. It is at least in part in what he *is*, in what he *does*, in what he seems *to wish to be*. The secret curriculum is the teacher's own lived values and convictions, in the lineaments of his expressions and in the biography of passion or self-exile which is written in his eyes.

Jonathan Kozol,
*The Night is Dark and
I am Far from Home*

spitwad *n* **1:** paper chewed and rolled into a ball to be thrown or shot as a missile

sutra *n* **1:** a precept summarizing ancient teachings **2:** a discourse of the Buddha

Contents

Acknowledgments

I have been fortunate to study and work with many great teachers, but I extend special thanks to Nereida Coulter, Victor Cozzalio, Marc Bertonasco, Donald Sturtevant, Victor Comerchero, Molly Irwin, Mary Giles, Wayne C. Booth, Joe Gill, Mike Mahlman, Dave Mahlman, Brother Ed, Brother Dan, Bill Cerney, Brother Tim, Tom English, Alan Howell, Mike Wenzel, Tom King, George Cotkin, and to all my colleagues in the English Department at Cal Poly, San Luis Obispo.

I also owe special thanks to Joel Beck and to the men of Vincent House, especially Eugene Clay, Roger Waxler, and Michael Price, for our many conversations about education, and to my friends Gary Cooper and Jim Cushing for their genius.

Introduction

What follows is the story of my initiation into the art of classroom teaching. It chronicles my transition from a graduate student at the University of Chicago, addicted to books and ideas, to an embattled ninth grade teacher—still addicted to books and ideas, but tempered by a new awareness of the difficulty of preserving their worth in the provincial, petty, sometimes even violent world of the American high school.

In this sense, my story is a kind of *Divine Comedy* in reverse, dramatizing my descent from an intellectual's heaven to an intellectual's purgatory—with my only guide and guru, my Virgil, a certain Brother Blake, a sixty-seven-year-old practitioner of the "pedagogy of the sublime."

To recount what he taught me about teaching and how he initiated me into its secret arts, I have assumed all the prerogatives of the novelist—altering names, combining characters, condensing time, and reinventing dialogue. If I have sometimes omitted too much or added events that took place only in my imagination, I have done so not out of irreverence or impudence but from the simple need to render Brother Blake's vision in the literary genres most capable of doing it justice: the legend, the memoir, and the philosophical dialogue.

Here, then, is a practitioner's confession, limited in scope and qualified by circumstance, that aspires, nevertheless, to serve as an intellectual survival manual for classroom teachers.

Spitwad Sutras

1

Vocation or Provocation?

He was at that age when, not yet knowing who he is, a man is ready to go whichever way a chance wind blows—into Persian Sufism or the unknown beginnings of Hungarian, the adventure of war or of algebra, Puritanism or the orgy.

Jorge Luis Borges, *The Anthropologist*

August 29, 1980

I never wanted to be a schoolteacher. I always had higher aspirations. In college, I wanted to be a famous writer, critic, or intellectual. I planned to study history, literature, and philosophy. And if by chance I ever ended up teaching, it would be strictly by accident—a spin-off of more serious pursuits. If I ever taught anybody anything, I imagined, it would be in the great tradition of Lao Tzu, Jesus, or the Buddha. And I would do it on television or in the streets—like Norman Mailer or Abbie Hoffman. I would never be trapped inside some building proctoring multiple-choice exams or nabbing cheaters who wrote the quadratic equation on the soles of their shoes. I would never become like my teachers—transparent instruments of bourgeois cultural values, poor slobs who couldn't even afford to buy a pair of stay-pressed pants.

And so, it was with profound humility, shame, and not a little nausea that I found myself five years after graduating from college walking down a red, pine-scented hallway, going to an interview for a job to teach ninth grade English at St. Vincent's Boy's Preparatory Academy, an orderly little school tucked inside a disintegrating lower-middle-class neighborhood in central California.

Taking that long walk past the trophy case in the echoing corridor brought back the tugs of a thousand minor emotions, none of them comfortable. I was twenty-seven years old and convinced that I was a complete failure. I had over $12,000 due in student loans, the final chapter of my dissertation to complete, and $47 worth of food stamps to my name. My nine-month-old marriage was hanging by a thread, and I had not yet altered the consciousness of my age. Hell, I hadn't even finished reading *Middlemarch*. And even if I got this job, in my own mind I still would not have a life. I would be a high school teacher in a "soft discipline"—what my dad used to call a "glorified baby-sitter."

The day I went for my interview, the students were on campus to register for their classes, and I must admit that they frightened me. Their wide eyes seemed capable of protean acts of moral repudiation. Teenage boys in dark sunglasses and $100 black canvas shoes would float by in groups of five or six. At first their arrogance and swagger appeared dangerous, wonderful, profound; at second glance, shallow, sentimental, and forced. Girls, visiting from nearby St. Theresa's Preparatory, bounced out of restrooms in bright pep squad uniforms as if emerging from time machines. Their youthful energy was undercut by the expressions on their faces: anxious, ambitious, contemporary.

Looking at those faces, trying to fathom their mysteries, I suddenly realized that American high schools are very hard to see. They are so permeated with myths and images from teenage exploitation films and bad television shows, so distorted in our memories by the excessive hopes and fears of our own adolescence, that they seem to shift and drift behind a kind of psychological fog.

I was glad finally to get inside the office. The secretary—a small woman in a modest white dress, Mrs. Gray—took me to a small conference room where vice principals conduct their interrogations. I was given a cup of instant coffee and told to wait.

Two faculty members who reminded me of off-duty police officers came in to interview me. They moved like athletes and had that same look of suppressed energy about the eyes. They asked me questions about my background, my teaching philosophy, how I would handle problem students, what I would do if somebody swore at me. Apparently it happens.

I lied, made things up, tried to sound like I knew something.

They could tell that I had no experience, that all my answers were suppositions, that I was, in fact, a displaced academic desperately in search of a job—any job. But they seemed to like the fact that I would say anything to get one. It indicated the kind of resourcefulness necessary to survive the ninth grade. It proved I could fight in clinches, that I wouldn't be held back by any false concessions to decorum.

Finally they asked me what I thought was the essence of Christianity. This was, after all, a Catholic school.

I said, "Love."

"Love?" they replied, eyebrows arched.

"Well, by love, I don't mean *gentleness!*" I said.

I got the job.

September

To my surprise, the first weeks of classes went smoothly. The students were uninspired but compliant. Those same dangerous boys that had frightened me in the hall were on guard in class, as mannered as they could manage to be. But I could tell they were unhappy. At that age, even pretenses are confessional. They were too serious. They answered my questions with solemnity and took out their pencils with excessive deliberateness. They were working very hard at suppressing their natural energy.

High school students, I found, are burdened, not so much by apathy, but by an unstoppable overflow of human reality, by the sheer preponderance of intimacy, hope, and fear welling up inside them and their peers. Life shouts at them from basketball hoops, fast-food restaurants, and expensive sweaters. There is such a rush and roar that academic subjects just sort of pale in its light and drown in its emotional tides.

But even though the young are rich in life, they live in fear of squandering their endowment. They worry about accumulating regrets or blowing opportunities—missing a dance, a party, or even a TV show. You can see it in their impatient eyes and hear it in the rise of their voices and the tap-tap-tapping of their pencils on their desks. They truly believe that youth is all there is, and this grandiose assumption—which almost no one in our culture dares to correct—burdens them more than we know, suffocating them with expectation.

Many of them even experience their own physical beauty as an alien visitation. I would find the boys in the restroom staring at their reflections, wondering, "I know I am sacred, but what does it mean?" No one tells them that youth is an illusion. No one even imagines that such a message might be, for some, a great consolation.

There were times upon entering the classroom when I would feel a swoon of compassion so profound that I truly did not see the violations of the dress code or the spitwads sailing across the room, and this rendered me an inept disciplinarian. All I could see was an ocean of lost souls totally outclassed by the sophisticated blandishments of fads, fashions, conformity, and infinite self-consciousness. All I could see were various versions of myself. And so, when they would fool around, I often just looked at them, fascinated by the details, as though I were peering into a mirror to examine the imperfections of my own face.

Many times I heard them ask one another impossible questions about sex, death, and injustice. Who killed Kennedy? Do boys ever really fall in love? Can Jesus save? And then they expected immediate answers, puzzled that their friends (who also possessed the holiness of youth) were so inarticulate, infantile, dumb. And yet anything I said about any of these subjects had to be run through the various filters of distrust, suspicion, and contempt that the living use to protect themselves from the effluvium of the dead.

Occasionally, after I had made what I thought was a particularly trenchant remark, I saw eyes look away from mine, not in reproach or disinterest, but in modesty—sensing that this particular life's revelation was not yet meant for them.

Still, who was I to complain? My students saw me exactly as they saw the rest of their teachers—as a necessary nuisance, a man who spoke for somebody other than himself. Friendly and admirable, the way a dentist is admirable. But certainly not an inspiration, certainly not a model, and definitely not Lao Tzu.

This saddened me a little, but it also seemed just. How could they take me any other way? I was not a healer but half a man who was only beginning to sense in their fragmented lives the completion of his own.

One of the privileges of teaching the ninth grade is that you get to witness moments of initiation in the lives of your young students—Joycean epiphanies that their parents never get to see and that the boys themselves never remember.

In my freshman humanities class, around the fourth week, we had an assignment to tell a joke in front of the other students. It was meant to be an icebreaker and introduction to public speaking. The boys were to rate each other on a scorecard for content, presentation, and organization.

As you might have guessed, the jokes were not very good. Short and stupid riddles, a few shaggy dog stories. What was interesting about this assignment was the way the students used it to establish a pecking order of daring and cool. The more risqué one's story, the more marginally obscene, the greater prestige one acquired from the class. "Tame" students told corny knock-knock jokes. "Live" students dared to offend.

Marlowe Lakes told the story of a prostitute who walked into a bar and told a man at the counter she would do anything he wanted for $50. The man told her, "Okay, paint my house."

When it was Teddy Latimer's turn, I expected a very tame story. Teddy was a quiet boy, slightly overweight and undernoticed. He seldom spoke in class. He always wore an undersized San Francisco Forty-Niners jacket torn at the pocket. His father was a nationally known avant-garde sculptor, and it seemed that Teddy was just biding his time. He seemed uninterested in showing off. So when he walked up to the front of the class with a confidence I had not seen in him before, I figured that he had a good joke, and I hoped the kids would listen to him.

"There was a man," he began, "who had this huge butt, and everywhere he went people would smell his big butt, and they'd all get sick and throw up!"

I didn't know quite how to respond to such fourteen-year-old humor. Had it been anyone else, I might have stopped him right there, but this was Teddy Latimer, who never risked anything, and yet he had decided to abjure all caution and go for the most fascinating story he could invent. He had decided to earn the respect of his peers through a performance in language and through a grand defiance of the teacherly censor. It was a one-boy free-speech movement, and the class responded with respectful silence, rapt attention, and an occasional guffaw.

Marlowe shouted out, "All right!"

And Marty Shuster began laughing so hard he slid under his desk.

"Teddy!" someone called in mock outrage.

And yet Teddy continued developing his story, embellishing it with ever-more-specific details.

"And this guy with the big butt fell in love with this girl with a bigger butt, and they wanted to have kids with big butts so they could send them to St. Vincent's High School and have them run for class president and do all the usual big-butt crap."

As he spoke, he gained more and more confidence.

"The problem was that this guy and this girl had kids with small butts. Tiny little crappers that wouldn't even fit on the end of a toilet seat!"

Well, to be honest, I can't remember the punch line to his story, but he went on like this for at least five minutes, making fun of the school, pushy parents, popularity, sports, and ending with a gentle poke at our school vice principal, Mr. Strapp, suggesting that his preoccupation with order and discipline had its source in severe potty training.

When Teddy walked back to his desk, the room rang with applause. I knew something had changed; he had passed some invisible teenage barrier and entered into the hierarchy of cool; he had ceased his isolation; he had taken a risk and earned the admiration of his peers.

I asked him to see me after class.

"Aww, Mr. Inchausti," he said, "I'm sorry if I said a few bad words, but I was talking to the guys, and, well, I just figured you'd understand, and if you didn't—well, I'm willing to take whatever punishment you want to give me." And he punctuated this brave talk by jutting out his little chin.

I told him that I thought he had a flair for storytelling, that he should get on the school newspaper or literary magazine. And then I handed him a copy of comedian Steve Martin's book of short stories, *Cruel Shoes*, which one of my friends had given me as a gift.

"Could you review this book for me?" I asked. "It's supposed to be funny."

A few days later, he stopped by after class, tossed the book at me, and gave me his assessment.

"It's okay," he said. "I like some of the stories, but they're not really funny; they're just kind of weird. I think to be funny, to make people laugh, you have to say things so real and true that they just sort of black out when they hear them."

"Interesting idea."

"I'm going to write stories like that someday," he said.

And then he walked out of the room with a little too much self-confidence.

Parents' night is a psychological multi-verse. The shadow sides of all your students suddenly appear in the form of grown-up caricatures—often antithetically split into male and female pairs. These animus-anima couplets sit on their sons' desks and ask you questions. Some of the desks are empty, and that seems symbolic too.

I begin negotiating a whole new set of authority issues. Who am I to these people? Don't they realize that *they* seem less real to me than their children, and yet they speak to me as if they are more real than their sons?

All of the parents are older than me. Most thank me for just staying in the same room with their teenage sons without running away. Others look at me with more suspicion than pity. "What exactly am I paying these tuition costs for?" they ask. "Can you tell me?"

Others want to know about the lives their children live when they are away from home.

"Does he speak up in class?"

"Is he sarcastic?"

"Does he have any friends?"

What do I know? I'm torn by my role as representative of the school—the teacher as public figure—and my own doubts about my capacities to teach anybody *any*thing.

I want to impress them with my professionalism, but I also want to burst out crying and confess everything. "Help me, help me! Who *are* these children? What can we do for them? I'm as lost as you are! Don't you hear the voices all around us? 'The horror, the horror!'"

I offer the parents an upbeat explanation of our program, yet I hate myself for being so affirmative, so confident. I feel like I'm part of a cover-up. The program here is as good as anywhere else. Better than most. At least that's what I keep telling myself.

Timmy's dad, owner of Snider Construction, asks me how much homework the kids should have every night, what Timmy is supposed to know at the end of the year, and what is the idea behind the daily journal entry.

I respond politely and intelligently. Everything seems to make sense—there is, after all a rationale for everything, a method behind every madness.

I show them their sons' journals. Some of them are appalled. The journals are messy, covered with slogans and pictures. Scrawl everywhere. Some have less than three prose entries.

"The kids can give as much or as little attention to these journals as they wish," I tell them. "It's a good index of how important writing is to them as a way of making sense of things. Some students have already written over twenty-five entries of thoughtful, probing prose. Others, as you can see, just doodle."

"How do you get them to move from nothing to something?" asks Mr. Snider.

Immediately I am stunned by the audacity of the question. As if I knew! I was only twenty-seven years old. What did I know? I hadn't a clue to the mysteries of human motivation; I was just their teacher. I assigned reading material and gave tests.

"I try to get them to experience the power of language." I say. "I give them assignments and hope they will get thirsty for more intellectual stimulation."

Mr. Snider looks at his son's drawing of a low-rider automobile with the caption "Vato Power" written above it. Then he looks up at me helplessly.

"It's what they do," I offer. "All the journals have stuff like that."

But it is no solace. I sense from him such disappointment, such heartbreak, that I know his dreams for his son must either be profound or terribly misguided. I really didn't know how to help him.

At around three o'clock every day, the students become inordinately conscious of the time. They sneak peeks at the clock every two to three minutes, groan, and more or less make life miserable for me and everyone else in the room until the final bell rings.

Yet after school, they crowd around my desk instead of going home.

"Hey?" I'd ask. "Two minutes ago, you were squirming in your chairs, waiting to get out of here; now that you're free, you stick around and bug me. What's the story?"

"That was *your* time," they'd say. "This is *ours*."

And strangely I knew what they meant. They hadn't chosen to be in class till 3:20—*that* time belonged to me. But they were

2

The Dialectics of Discipline

Human beings—human children especially—seldom deny themselves the pleasure of exercising a power which they are conscious of possessing, even though that power consists only in a capacity to make others wretched; a pupil whose sensations are duller than those of his instructor, while his nerves are tougher and his bodily strength perhaps greater, has an immense advantage over that instructor, and he will generally use it relentlessly, because the very young, very healthy, very thoughtless, know neither how to sympathize nor how to spare.

Charlotte Brontë, *The Professor*

October

My teacher's honeymoon, however, didn't last very long. About the third week, things began to unravel. I realized this when Marlowe Lakes tossed Marty Shuster's book bag out the window. Cliques were forming. They were beginning to abuse one another and to make fun of the weaker kids. Even James Bailey, the pride of the debate team, was late three days in a row.

Slowly, all the fragile conventions and class rules that I had managed to put into place were being challenged. This growing resistance seemed to be moving toward open revolt, and yet I could see no way of stopping it. The mood of the class and my own fragile authority were about to collide, and I sat there helpless to prevent the impending crash—both bystander and victim, bracing myself for the impact.

In the teacher's lounge, I blamed President Reagan, I blamed television, I blamed their parents, the economic system, modernism, postmodernism, new math. But as accurate as my analyses were, I was still living inside that classroom, confronted every day by its oppressive intimacies and its growing instabilities. Theory alone could not save me, and blaming others was no solace.

My one hope was that the students had yet to realize where things were heading, and this gave me a little time. But what could I do?

Each day now, about two hours before going to school, I felt a hollow terror in the pit of my stomach and my arms felt strangely light, as if beginning to disconnect from my body. My usual symptoms of panic.

I started to enforce class rules more strictly. If anyone acted up, I sent him immediately to the vice principal's office. One Thursday, I sent seven students to the office. That afternoon, the vice principal called me downstairs for a private conference.

Mr. Strapp, dean of discipline, was an intense man with incredible energy and a gift for intimidating oratory. He stood about five feet, seven inches tall and wore a buzz cut and pink polyester shirt—a poor man's Robert Conrad. He had thin lips but big eyes, and when he got mad, accusations could fly from his lips with machine-gun rapidity. A former member of the U.S. Marine Corps, Strapp was the disciplinary terror of the school.

"Now, exactly what did these boys do?" he asked me.

"Well, they were disruptive, talked out of turn, threw paper, that sort of thing." I expected Strapp to agree that these boys needed to learn how to behave, and so I was surprised to find him telling me—quite to the contrary—that these disciplinary problems were not severe, that they should be dealt with in the classroom, and that *he* had larger responsibilities.

"I guess I just assumed that my job was to teach and your job was to keep discipline," I said. But Strapp just ignored my pitiful accusation.

"Yes, you've got to handle these things yourself. I know you're new, and you don't really know how to do it yet. Just keep them after school, call their parents. But *don't send them down to my office* unless something really outrageous happens. And I mean *outrageous*: injuries, fights, weapons, that sort of thing."

Then Strapp went right to what he considered to be the heart of the matter. "Mr. Inchausti, do you have a deep need to be liked?"

The question flabbergasted me. "I don't think so, sir. I have a family that provides me with the emotional support I need. I have friends. I don't think the affection of my students is overwhelmingly important to me."

Strapp accepted my answer as the usual evasive crap—the typical denial of a compassionate weakling.

"You didn't expect me to be so direct, did you?" he said. "I've seen all this before. Young teacher, soft heart, you want to be their buddy. They act up, and you overreact. It's common. I'll work with you on it."

Who was he kidding? He didn't want to *work with me* on this; he wanted me to go away.

He stared at me as if we then shared an intimate knowledge of my secret shame of wanting to be loved too much—as if he had penetrated to the source of all this bother.

I searched inside for some confirmation of his accusation, but there was none. And so that look of certainty on Strapp's face—a gloat really—struck me as incredibly facile, and I hated him for it. But I could tell I had already taken up too much of his time, so I just left the room—seething.

The next day, Strapp showed up in my classroom to "help out with the discipline problem."

"Uh, excuse me, Mr. Inchausti, but *do you mind* if I address your class?"

"No, go right ahead."

"Thank you."

Strapp's presence was weighty. The floor seemed to tilt in his direction, the carpet sagged, the walls bent forward, the barometric pressure increased, you could hear the faint buzz of the General Electric wall clock.

Strapp used the dramatic pause masterfully. He toyed with his audience, playing on their fears, looking around at the class as if searching for the exact place to begin, the exact spot from which to get a fingernail hold to rip away their facade of innocence and reveal the real-world demons behind it.

And then, looking away for a moment, as if giving up the search, his voice snuck back into the room.

"Now, I know that some of you think you've got A PRETTY GOOD THING going here, but I'm here to tell you THAT IT IS GOING TO STOP, AND IT IS GOING TO STOP NOW!"

The class went stiff, trying to stop doing the nothing that they were already doing. No one dared look up.

He paused again to find his motivation, to let the anger fill, perhaps just to watch them squirm. And then he began again, from the top.

"All this talking, fooling around, fighting, I'VE HAD ENOUGH OF IT!"

There was a brief pause as everyone took this in.

"Now, we've got a few new teachers here this year, and they're doing a good job. Mr. Inchausti does not have to come here every day and work with you. Yet you take advantage of him, and I am SICK OF IT! SICK AND TIRED OF YOUR COWARDLY BE-HAVIOR!"

He looked around the room now in a masterful display of fearless moral outrage. One by one, the students avoided eye contact with him by looking down at their desks. This seemed to calm him for a moment.

"Now, if you have a problem with Mr. Inchausti, if you think he is not being fair with you, TALK WITH HIM AFTER CLASS! And if you still feel an injustice exists, that somehow he is not getting the message, that your little problems are not being adequately addressed—then, and only then, come and see me, and we'll work something out."

"BUT IF I EVER HEAR that ONE of Mr. Inchausti's students has been sent to my office—that one of you has interrupted one of his lessons—then, Gentlemen, HEAVEN HELP YOU, because I AM NOT GOING TO TOLERATE IT ANYMORE!"

At this point, he slapped his palm upon the desk, and the resulting pop made several of the kids jump. I wondered if anyone had wet his pants.

Strapp glanced over to me as if to say, "See? This is how you do it."

"Now, I'm going to give the class back to Mr. Inchausti," he said. "And I HOPE THAT YOU ALL HAVE LEARNED SOME-THING!"

He left as quickly as he had arrived and walked swiftly down the hall, as if he had just completed a rather burdensome, if simple, task—like installing a new fan belt in his car.

After he was gone, my class relaxed, but nobody spoke for a long while. It was like the calm one feels after having thrown up—grateful that it's over but cautious, knowing that the illness just might return.

This mood was broken when Ben Brown boldly announced: "That old windbag, he don't scare me!"

Now, I was put in a bind. I couldn't send Ben down to the office and risk having Strapp consider me a poor disciplinarian again, but I really wasn't capable yet of offering a stinging reply of my own.

"Ben," I said, "that's enough. Mr. Strapp was not trying to scare you; he was trying to *educate* you. He wants you to grow up."

It was the best I could do, but after any encounter with Strapp, I always found myself saying asinine things.

Ben could not let me get away with it.

"Oh, yeah? If he's trying to educate me, then what's that old noisemaker gotta yell for and get all upset and weird for, huh?"

And although I agreed with what Ben said, I found myself strangely bound by adult loyalty to Strapp.

"Okay, Ben, go stand outside of class until the period is over, and see me after school."

"But Mr. Inchausti, I was just . . ."

"Never mind, Ben, go."

I opened the door to let Ben out, and I saw Strapp standing at the end of the hall. He was surprised to see me. He obviously had turned his thoughts to other matters, and I could tell by the furrow in his brow that he was not pleased that I was kicking one of my students out of class so soon after his lecture.

When I ducked back into the classroom, someone had thrown Todd's books out the window. And on the chalkboard was a picture of a witch with exaggerated breasts labeled "Mr. Strapp." Behind the witch, riding on her broom, was a little cat wearing a name tag that read "Mr. Inchausti."

I was beginning to think that my whole life had taken a wrong turn, that I didn't belong here, that it was just all too petty and wearisome. A mind like mine was wasted in the classroom. Lao Tzu would not have put up with any of this.

And yet perhaps the students were right. Maybe I was a pussycat after all, Strapp's feline familiar.

If that was so, then maybe I was also endowed with secret animistic powers of transformation.

But how was I to gain access to them? What was I to do? Howl at the moon?

Mike Morton, the history teacher in the room next to mine, was always getting into trouble for his unsound methods. But as wild as he seemed to be, I was always learning from him.

He would lambast his classes with thirty-minute harangues while they pretended not to be listening.

"You know you run this school, that no one makes you think," he'd say. "And yet you believe that when you get out of here someday that somehow, some way, you're going to make a million dollars. Well, it doesn't work that way."

There was one incident in particular that I remember: Morton walks up to a student who is slouching at his desk—Butch Atkins, the 210-pound tackle on that year's football team—and says "Look at this guy. How is he going to get anything done if he's not *erect*?"

A few students in the class laugh, and Butch becomes aroused.

"Shut up, Morton," he says, "or I am going to stick this wad of bubble gum in your freaking beard."

"Butch," Morton replies, "if that is the only way you can express yourself, you are in worse shape than I thought."

Then Butch takes the bubble gum out of his mouth, loads it up in his right hand, and makes his way toward Morton.

Morton decides that if Butch comes within two feet of him, he will bury his fist into Butch's jaw, just to the right of that little scar below the lip.

But instead of placing the gum in Mike's beard, Butch charges Morton, blocking him like a football player and bouncing him up against the blackboard.

Morton finds himself suspended against the wall, pinned by Butch's huge forearm. He manages to croak out a warning, "Put me down."

Butch looks at Mike, trying to figure out who this guy is. Morton had to be a loser or he wouldn't have let Butch do this to him, yet Butch can see that Morton really is not afraid of him. Even in that silly posture, Morton still seems to possess an authority that Butch does not have. What in hell is it?

Butch finally lets Morton go and walks quietly back to his desk, sitting down as if nothing had happened.

Morton feels in control now, as if this charade of violence is something he himself has concocted to refocus the classroom energies. He feels no need to send Butch to the principal. The "fight" seems to have cleared the air in some occult way. The students are now more attentive, Butch Atkins far less pained.

Mike, of course, could speak to few people about the incident. If the administrators had gotten wind of it, Butch would have been suspended, Mike reprimanded, but little would have been done to clarify what had really taken place.

It is difficult to find anyone willing to think through the emotional dynamics of an event like this, although they happen in classes more often than we care to admit. Everyone is quick to explain it, or manage it, but no one is willing to examine it as some extreme lesson in the dynamics of classroom authority.

And yet that is exactly what Mike Morton considered the event to have been. His role, he had decided, was to ponder and unlock the meaning of such classroom occurrences, which he termed "postmodern effects." "Postmodern effects" were problems, he believed, that transcended his little classroom and our little school. They were indicative of a future already upon us. And if a student had almost beaten him up—well, that meant that somewhere, some other teacher was probably receiving worse, so one had to take one's problems as emblematic of the times and not personalize them.

Mike told me that, every so often, a student would subject him to a "hate stare."

"They usually sit back in their desks, backs straight, and stare at you without moving—letting you know, in a wordless way, exactly how much they loathe you. I usually ignore such challenges, but for some reason, one day, I just couldn't take it anymore. So, I walked up to the student—it was Buck Bonomi—and told him, 'Go ahead, say it!'

"Buck was silent and morose. He knew passivity was his best weapon—hell, his only weapon.

"So I said, 'Okay, I'll say it for you.' And while looking directly in his eyes, I said, 'Screw you!'"

"Do you think that was wise?" I asked.

"I had to make him conscious of what he was doing. Buck understood that he was assaulting me, but he thought he was safe, hidden, underground. He had discovered a cowardly way to fight me, and so I had to call him on it. I had to show him that no one is invisible, that his intentions were transparent, that he couldn't count on my 'civility' to protect him.

"By the end of the quarter, we were close friends, and he was less of a coward."

I didn't know how much of this to believe.

"We don't know how to teach them," Mike would say. "And they don't know how to learn from us. So they use us as foils to figure out the system, in hopes that they'll never have to grow up.

And we don't confront them about this, because we don't have any alternatives to the system. The only thing we offer them is the intolerable option of becoming like us!"

Such stinging self-accusations, of course, were only half true—but that half truth was a powerful one. I knew that it was as hard for Mike to admit that we were in over our heads as it was for anyone else, and so his words moved me, not to pity, but to a kind of grudging admiration for this strange, extreme man.

"Then why do you stay?" I asked.

"Someone has to be here for these kids," he said. "And someone has got to think seriously about *this circus* from the inside out. Besides, our task is not to change them, so much as to *survive them*. Only then do we become their teachers: heroic counterexamples to their unexamined lives."

I took my wife, Linda, to the school dance. I was assigned to chaperon.

The gym had been transformed by the darkness into a cavern. There were a few shabby decorations, one poster, five streamers, a table with sore-throat punch, and a dozen small Dixie Cups. No doubt the work of the sophomore class.

Several girls from Saint Theresa's huddled together, talked intensely for a few minutes, and then one of them would sprint across the room. The boys immediately moved much more slowly, talked less. One of them was a prince—the subject of all the girls' conversations. He stood apart from the others, leaning against the wall, as if to allow everyone to take full measure of his Dionysian aura.

Next to me was a parent chaperon, Mrs. McGowen. Her twelfth grade son was "somewhere around here." She seemed a bit nervous. Was she terrified or ecstatic? I couldn't tell. She was slim and tastefully dressed in a tweed blazer. She told me she was a child and family counselor, but I could tell she didn't want to talk. She had many things on her mind. Her eyes searched the dance floor, looking for God knows what.

Teenage couples came up to her, and she chatted with them, expressing interest and encouragement. "Oh? And are you going out for a drive after the dance? Be *careful*!"

I had darker intimations of the intentions of these kids but smiled and nodded anyway. Linda wanted to dance, but I was watching Marlowe Lakes. He was probably hatching some plot involving a six-pack hidden in the trunk of his big brother's car. He seemed to understand all this better than I did. He seemed to like it here.

I looked at my watch. I had been at the dance only twenty minutes. Suddenly, I was engulfed by a profound wave of depression, and I didn't know why. The band took a break, the lights got brigher, everything turned uglier, and I told Linda I had to go home.

"Are you sick?" she asked.

"Yes, I'm sick. Sick of this dance! Sick of this job! Sick of everything! What am I doing here in this unholy marriage of heavy-metal dreams and pink party decorations? Am I expected to be the happy patron? Or suspicious cop? Am I supposed to be the designated cheerful idiot? I'm sorry, Linda, I *cannot* endure this gracefully. I *cannot* endure it at all!"

"You take things too personally!"

"No, not personally," I insisted. "I take them seriously. There's a difference."

"It's only a dance," she replied.

"No," I said, not caring how melodramatic I sounded. "It's my *life*! This dance has become my job, and my job has become my life!"

"You need to get out of here," she said, and within minutes we were in the car, negotiating the poorly lit streets, talking about my "problem" and whether or not Strapp had noticed that we had left early.

"Look," I told her. "I am struggling here with the idea that I just might be called to be a teacher. But at that dance, I saw that being a teacher also means being a kind of odd fellow, and it simply galls me. Do I have to go to all these damn dances and football games? Do I have to organize fund drives and police the cloakrooms? Does all this come with the territory?"

The horror of the provincial and the petty—the very things that had driven me to books and ideas in the first place—were now all around me, demanding to be recognized, demanding to be served!

"I don't know," Linda said. "It seems like all this *does* come with the job."

"Then what can I do?" I asked, not expecting any answer.

"Not everyone is troubled by these things," she said. "Is it really so bad?"

I just looked out the car window. No, it wasn't *so* bad. It just wasn't what I was put on earth to do. And it was getting late enough in my life that I didn't want to endure any more false starts. But I couldn't tell if my insistence on finding a meaningful vocation was simply a form of self-indulgence or my last link to the truth—the one thing that made it possible for me to hope in the future.

I had promised myself in college that I would never allow myself to be swallowed up by the insipid, the inane, or the inessential. Could I hold out? *Should* I hold out?

A candy apple–red pickup truck with oversized tires, driven by the same kids who had been talking to Mrs. McGowen, passed by our car. It weaved in and out of traffic, shot past the Ship of Zion Baptist Church, and then powered down a dark side street, a diet cola can flying out the side window.

No! I wasn't wrong. I would quit, find another job. There were better ways to make a living than to serve as a patsy for these spoiled children.

3

Breakthrough

God instructs the heart—not by means of new ideas but by pains and contradictions.
>   —Father J. P. deCaussade, S. J., *Self-Abandonment to Divine Providence*

October

I gave up trying to solve my discipline problem. It was just too much for me. I simply accepted a degree of chaos in my classes, plodded along from day to day, and starting looking for other work.

At this time, my class took up the study of the New Testament parables. And although I tried to convince my students—when they were paying attention—that these stories possessed rich and complex teachings, they insisted upon seeing them as expressing only the most tired moral platitudes.

"No, no," I insisted. "There is nothing in these stories telling us to *be good!* The point seems to be exactly the opposite; God does what he pleases!"

But they were not intrigued by what they took to be my feigned heresy and considered my questions merely as some sort of trick to get them to do more work.

When I asked Jim Bailey to read the parable of the sower, he read with exaggerated religiosity in a voice like Billy Graham. This brought laughter from the back of the class, and I found myself strangely relieved to find that someone was paying *that* much attention. I knew I wasn't teaching them anything, so I was grateful for the good humor.

Every day, I would go home and replay classroom incidents over and over again in my mind. There was something in the complacent way Marty Shuster had interpreted the parable of the sower as indicating that we should all "love God" that struck me as the very thing I was put on earth to eliminate. It was not my students' ignorance that was so exasperating, nor was it their rowdy behavior; it was the audacity of their small minds and the power their pettiness possessed to undermine everything in life that I valued. Why were these kids so certain that there was nothing important they could learn *from me*, when one look *at them*, one walk down the damn school hallway, provoked so many revelations in my mind that I could barely process them all?

Each night, I would talk myself into new resolves by planning innovative lessons and novel approaches. But the next day, my enthusiasm would dry up when I saw their tired expressions. Sometimes, when I talked to that wall of disengaged faces, I would end up listening to myself and forgetting why I was talking. It was as if my mind was floating about three feet to the side of my body, unable to get back inside my head. It was an awful feeling, and when it happened I would often just stop talking and sit down while the students would talk to one another about nothing.

One day, I read aloud to them from Matthew 13: the passage on why Jesus taught with parables. The text rang out in complete harmony with my mind:

> You will listen and listen again, but not understand, see and see again, but not perceive. For the heart of this nation has grown coarse, their ears are dull of hearing, and they have shut their eyes for fear they should see with their eyes, hear with their ears, understand with their hearts, and be converted and healed by me.

My forehead tingled. I felt like a prophet. These were *my* words now. Both a challenge and confession. All my past intellectual training, graduate school, my late night self-study of Gramsci and Lacan, seemed but a prelude to this moment. Everything I ever knew or believed seemed contained in these lines, and all my aspirations as an educator poured into those last seven words: "and be converted and healed by me."

But my students were not impressed. This passage didn't seem such a revelation to them. If anything, it was an insult—an accusation, a prelude, no doubt, to more homework or staying after school. I could see it in the way Teddy Latimer doodled with his San Francisco Giants pencil, in the way Marty Shuster looked deeply into his notebook, and in the way Jim Bailey sat upright and petrified.

But I hadn't intended it to be accusatory. I saw the lines as an invitation to change, as encouragement to overthrow the past, as an incitement to see, to hear, to feel anew, to be a part of a new heaven and earth. I was reaching for my messianic moment, but no one was there.

"This passage," I said, "shows us how Jesus taught. He taught with authority, not like the scribes. Jesus didn't threaten people. He liberated them so that they could see with their own eyes, hear with their own ears, and understand with their own hearts."

I was attempting to model this authority myself, trying to enact the role of Christ the Liberator. I had no idea then how vain and presumptuous I must have appeared until a spitwad, very wet and traveling at high speed, suddenly struck the center of my forehead.

I flinched. I heard laughter. Jeers. Shouts of triumph.

And then, almost simultaneously, the bell rang, signaling the end of school.

By the time I regained my composure, it was too late. My classroom was empty. All of my students had run out the door.

Now, I could have gotten on the public address system and called them back. I could have waited until later and called all their parents on the telephone. I could have done a lot of things, but nothing seemed to really address the issue.

Sure, I might be able to gain power over these kids. I even might be able to compel them to behave. But I could never force them to learn from me or to care about the things I loved. Besides, who was I to model Christ? Maybe I should adopt the drill instructor strategy that seemed to work so well for Strapp? Maybe that man did know something about education after all? Maybe this whole idea of setting the mind free had to wait until these adolescents had been decanted of some of their sexual energy? Maybe I was just dead wrong about everything? Maybe I was, in fact, just a very silly man?

As I sat at my desk with these thoughts spinning in my mind, someone entered the room. When I looked up, I saw sixty-seven-year-old Brother Blake standing there, his large tummy pushing out his black Christian Brother's robe. He looked like a black dolphin with snow white hair.

"Well," he said, his eyes twinkling, "you look like you've had a good day."

I didn't want to tell him what had happened, but some flicker of intelligence in his face reassured me that there was little he had not seen of classroom fiascoes, so I blurted out everything—my speech, the spitwad, my inaction and resentments—everything. To my relief, Blake was not shocked, nor did he tell me to "get tough."

Most teachers, I found, seldom admit to the psychological horrors in their classrooms or to misgivings about their teaching skills to anyone but a few trusted souls. They do this in self-defense because they are so often blamed for anything that goes wrong. This is why many teachers are upbeat to the point of hyperactivity and stay that way until they can no longer ignore the discrepancy between their positive attitude and the darker realities of their profession. That is when they burn out, quit, start selling real estate, turn cynical or fanatically idealistic, write books, run for the school board, or become administrators. So I was relieved when Brother Blake took my confession not as a sign of personal inadequacy but as an objective description of an entirely logical chain of events.

"Sounds like somebody was listening to your talk on authority," he said.

"What do you mean?" I asked.

"Someone sent you a message about authority."

"And what might that message be?" I asked.

"That *you don't have it!*"

The remark hurt. I knew it was true, but it was still painful to hear.

"But then how do I *get* authority?" I asked.

"For starters, don't resent the kids for pointing out the truth. You tell them to seek truth, don't you? No matter how difficult that truth might be? So don't duck it yourself. You *don't* have authority, but that doesn't mean you will *never* have it. The important thing right now is just to *see* the destruction of your own pretenses and posturing. It's the only way to move from fearing nothing to realizing that there is nothing to fear."

"That's fine advice, Brother," I countered, "but I have to deal with these kids again tomorrow, and I've lost their respect. How am I to teach them about parables? What do I do? Pretend nothing happened?"

"Tell them the parable of the teacher who got hit between the eyes with a spitwad. Ask *them* what it means."

I could tell by the look on his face that he had just given me one of his keys to classroom success: The trick was in providing a link between what the students were feeling and the lesson at hand, and then giving oneself over to the messy process through which that link is explored, expounded, and finally understood. To do this, however, required that you take a risk, leave the lesson open, discover its meaning as you proceeded. Teaching was more like chasing down a metaphor or solving an equation than it was like giving a speech or dispensing information.

I could feel the anxiety melt from my neck and arms and a new anticipatory energy surge within me. His approach just might work. Besides, what had I to lose? The problems of today invent the lessons of tomorrow. There was little else the teacher had to know except the endless varieties of human evasion and perversion as they clashed with the wisdom of one's discipline in the microcosm of the classroom. Errors and miscalculations were part of the lesson, and the subject matter was one with its troubled transmission.

"Youth," Blake said, "with all its anarchic energy, impertinence, and physical beauty, is just God's gift to the inane and immature. Don't resent it; its all they've got."

I began to get my confidence back: being locked up in the ninth grade may not be such a bad destiny after all. I had never thought to connect literature to life in so direct a fashion. I had never thought to see problems as metaphors—emblematic of their own solutions. I wondered how I could have studied for so long and came to know so little.

A teacher was not a scholar or policeman or glorified baby-sitter. A teacher was more like Virgil or Odysseus: a creature of dialogue. An embodied phantom. Imagination incarnate. Not the Holy Spirit, but its secular double—with one finger pointed resolutely across the cultural abyss at the sacred face of the moon.

The next day, following silent prayer, I announced to the class that I wanted them to interpret a parable. "It's the story of the teacher who got hit between the eyes with a spitwad."

They braced themselves; no one looked me in the eye. Marty started to fidget.

"There was once a teacher who wanted to teach about authority," I began. "Not the authority of power or position, but real authority—the kind one earns through insight and accomplishment. And as he talked about this, a spitwad came out of nowhere and hit him right between the eyes. Before he could do anything, the students ran out of the room. And he was left alone and humiliated." I paused for a moment, and then asked, "Now, what might this story mean?"

No one spoke for a long time, until Marty Shuster raised his hand. "It means that we should respect our teachers and not abuse them."

"No, it doesn't mean *that*!" I snapped, not without a little disgust. "That's not what the story is about! A few days ago, I taught you that one way to unravel a parable is first to isolate the images and then assign them values. Now, who could the teacher be?"

"You."

"Who are the students?"

"We are."

"What is the spitwad?"

There was a brief silence; then everyone had an answer.

"Anger," said Jim Bailey.

"Contempt," said Marlowe Lakes.

"No, fun," shouted Ben Brown.

"Freedom," "power," "truth," "honesty." Concepts came from everywhere, but there were too many to sort out, so I stopped brainstorming and just grabbed one.

"Okay, if the spitwad stands for truth, what is the parable saying?"

Marty Shuster offered his first real idea of the year. "If the spitwad is truth, then the teacher was the one who learned the lesson. He got the truth in his face when he was pretending he already had it in his head."

"But if the teacher is trying to tell the truth," Jim Bailey argued, "then the spitwad must stand for something having to do with students refusing the truth."

"Maybe," offered Marlowe, "truth has nothing to do with it. Maybe the story is about how kids and teachers make contact. Those contacts aren't anything like what teachers want them to be, and that's why teachers pretend to be mean all the time."

I was astounded. We were doing first-class literary criticism now, and my students were actually interested in the debate! Was I finally asking the right questions? Was my two-step strategy for interpreting parables the key? Or was it the risk I took in allowing the discussion to go beyond what I knew? Were my students aware of how profound their answers were? It was hard to tell, but there was no doubt that I had done something right this time.

Such self-congratulatory reflections took my attention from the rear of the classroom just long enough for someone to drop Stevie

Chamber's books out the window. The discussion lost its focus, then its energy. But it didn't matter. I had begun to learn my craft.

What that craft *was*, I was uncertain. What I was learning about it, even less certain. Still, I was onto something important here, and I wasn't going to leave this place until I figured out what it was.

4

The Lost Art

Education is not sermonizing to children against their instincts and pleasures, but providing a natural continuity between what they feel and what they can and should be. But this is a lost art.

Allan Bloom, *The Closing of the American Mind*

November

"For some reason," Brother Blake told me, "the kids just love to throw paper. I had the same problem as you did when I first started teaching. At first, I would just compliment the offender, telling him, 'Good, that's right! You are looking for power. But you are looking for it in the wrong place. Its not in spitwads, it's in words! Seek word power, not paper power! Throw words!'

"But they didn't listen. So, one day, I hit upon the idea that I would just let them throw spitwads at one another until they dropped. I picked a Friday before a vacation, when there would be little work to do anyway, and I told them they could throw paper at one another for as long as they wished, provided they stopped ten minutes before the end of class to clean up the mess. They thought it was a great deal, and so the paper began to fly. Somewhere in the back of my mind, I suspected that after twenty or thirty minutes, they would find throwing paper tiresome and inane. But I was wrong. The more paper they threw, the more paper they *wanted* to throw.

"The classroom began to fill up with debris. They emptied their binders of every available scrap of paper, and they began to throw paper *at me*. They were totally out of control. I was frightened and horrified but tried hard not to show it. They would corner one of their friends in the back of the room and, with glee in their eyes, bounce a wad of paper as big as your fist off his head with all the power and violence they could muster, then break out in squeals of delight.

"Ten minutes before the bell rang, I asked them to clean up the room. They did a kind of general sweep of the floor but left thousands of pieces of paper scattered about. The event had effected no catharsis whatsoever; in fact, it made them even harder to control.

" 'We'll clean up the rest of the paper, Brother Blake, if you let us throw spitwads after vacation,' they said.

"I was stunned. The more I gave, the more they took. Their capacity for effrontery was endless, and I concluded that my little experiment in excess was one of the stupidest things I had ever done.

"Or so I thought. A year or two later, I was teaching ninth grade English again, and one of the students shot a spitwad across the room. Our eyes met, and a very odd thing happened. As I looked at him, I could see that he knew that I knew more about spitwads than he did, that I'd been through spitwad hell, and that his sorry excuse for a spitwad did not impress me in the least. But more importantly, his behavior did not frighten me as it would have that first year, because I was no longer paralyzed by my own dread as to where his actions might lead. I knew where they could lead. I knew the inner dynamics of classroom chaos better than anyone, because I had already experienced its extremes.

"Before that moment, I never thought that wasted period two years ago had taught me anything, but I was wrong. It had given me an edge, a little extra confidence, a little extra knowledge of what could happen that only an experienced teacher possesses. That brave journey into the heart of spitwad darkness had given me authority, real classroom authority that I could have gained in no other way. And, you know, after looking into my eyes, that little rascal never shot another spitwad.

"That same year, my class simply stopped working two weeks before Christmas vacation. At first, I was outraged by their lack of discipline, until I realized that what was really upsetting me was not their behavior, but my inability to change it. I just could not admit to myself that I did not know how to motivate them, that I wasn't as great a teacher as I thought I was, that there were things I didn't know—that there were things *no teacher knew*.

"Once I owned up to my own imperfection, the class did not bother me as much; it fascinated me. Instead of dreading being in the room with those manipulative kids, I actually almost looked forward to being there to watch them, to see exactly how they resisted work and how they played me off against myself, to watch my own reactions to them, and to fathom the dynamics of class-room insincerity and bogus participation.

"I began to catalog their intellectual evasions. I never took anything they did personally, but I did take it seriously—as a specimen of intellectual rebellion. In fact, this process worked so well that I decided to give up all my cherished notions about education altogether and just watch for my failures. I did this for ten years. It was my cross, my destiny, my power. It became my way."

Blake was silent for a while, looking off in the distance. "When I was younger," he said, "teaching was a kind of game to me. I could afford to take it lightly, because my real life was elsewhere. My real life was in the way I opened doors and tossed myself on the table in front of the room—my real life was my youth!

"Besides, it was fun to be young and have a profession. I played one off the other in a kind of lighthearted dance. No one really expected me to know what I was doing, and, on the other hand, no one really expected me to be so smart. I couldn't lose!

"But now I don't have youth, and my life has become my work. It is as if, in playing at having a vocation, I acquired one. And so now, when I walk into a class, I still toss myself up on the table, but that is no longer what I am there for. I am there to capture and articulate what is *out there*—the creative revelations pulsating in the air. They are what I live for now. What else have I got?"

I asked Brother Blake what to do when the students keep talking after the bell rings.

"Wait for them," he said. "They are not ready to start yet."

"But they will talk all period!"

"No they won't. Just wait. They will be silent within three minutes."

I was skeptical, but I tried it the next day, and it worked. Without my saying anything, the class stopped talking within two minutes, looked up from their desks, and were ready to begin. I was amazed.

"Why does it work?" I asked him.

"When you are patient, you communicate your respect for them. And unless you have totally lost their trust, they will reciprocate. It's only natural."

Not everyone was as impressed with Brother Blake's methods as I was. In fact, Strapp had already formed a committee to look into getting rid of the interdisciplinary humanities program that Blake had designed and go back to three separate courses in English, social science, and religion. The coaches were on his side, along with some of the parents and alumni.

Brother Blake's program, they said, simply lacked any objective measures by which to assess its achievements. It was too subjective. High schools were not built for this kind of education.

But I sensed that Strapp's suspicions of Brother Blake went even deeper than his dislike of the curriculum. You could see it in the way he would bristle whenever Brother Blake would raise philosophical questions at department meetings. Strapp was a practical man. He was interested in meeting the needs of the parents—his clientele—not in some mystagogic interpretation of high school as a living laboratory in philosophical anthropology.

"Teach the basics," Strapp would say. "Teach them effectively. The students will at least know their capitals, read a few short stories, write in complete sentences, spell. That's enough! In fact, that's damn good!"

Brother Blake's approach, I was told, had just confused everything.

Blake and Strapp, I decided, were just two decidedly different kinds of Catholics—indeed, two radically different kinds of men, the mystic and the man of action. Strapp's point was clear: there is a side of life that is not complex or difficult, a side that is straightforward and yields to a strong will. And that obvious side is the side of life we must take on. The rest—literature, ideas, philosophy—distract us from the tough, straight-ahead task of accomplishing the expected. For young boys, abstractions were pure poison, paralyzing the will at the very moment of its inception. What they needed was direction and a *tempering* of the imagination, not incitement to reflection!

But I was not convinced. Brother Blake seemed to be the only person in that school with a realistic assessment of what took place in the classroom, the only one not hiding behind clichés, the only one still intellectually alive. The obvious needs of our students were not so obvious at all. What the parents wanted for their sons was not necessarily what we, in good conscience, should provide.

Brother Blake saw his version of education going back at least as far as the great Mesopotamian and Egyptian mythologies—those first attempts to articulate a spiritual world and lift humanity out of the primordial womb of nature into the life of the mind. For Blake, our adolescent students were still living that primordial existence, most of them still fascinated by the warrior *geist* of the barbarian hordes of prehistory. And our task as teachers was to bring them into the more humane vision of the tribal mythologies as precursor to their tragic initiation into civilization. Teaching ninth grade, according to Brother Blake, was largely the task of spiritualizing the natural man—laying the foundations for some future Age of Greece.

Blake told me, "Mr. Strapp is always asking me how can we better prepare these kids for college. And I tell him that he's asking the wrong question. College professors have a very different job than we do. They take our brightest students and show them how little they really know. They initiate the young into the art of thinking against themselves. Our task is to initiate them into being affirmative. Its a very different thing.

"Have you ever seen those straight-A students who go directly to college and get straight A's there, but yet never experience the *metanoia* or 'turn' that constitutes authentic intellectual awakening? They had high school teachers that 'prepared' them for college—that is to say, inoculated them against radical self-examination. I want my students to go to college more passionate than prepared, less defended and more willing to risk failure. There is nothing more obtuse than a self-satisfied college freshman with high SAT scores and narrow careerist ambitions.

"Students need a perspective that allows them to continue to be transformed, changed, and renewed by their experiences. Ultimately, we want them to surprise us by their futures, not live out some ambitious high school administrator's dream of a successful life."

I decided that I would follow Blake's lead regardless of the warnings. For as hardheaded as Strapp seemed, his will to discipline bred self-righteousness and sentimentality in those who embraced it. I could see it in the coaches and their following of dependent, once delinquent boys. Besides, Strapp's discipline-through-terror strategy had not brought any real order to my class—nor had it made me a better teacher.

Yet, I also knew that if there was to be a struggle over the curriculum, Strapp and the forces for a return to basics would probably win. And I wondered if I could teach in a program designed by people like them. Blake's existential pedagogy of the sublime had inspired me.

5

Classroom Praxis from A to B

In all my lectures I have taught one doctrine—namely the infinitude of the private man. . . . I gain my point, gain all points, whenever I can reach the young with any statement which teaches them their own worth.

Ralph Waldo Emerson

November

Try as I might, I was unable to apply Brother Blake's approach to my own classes. The students would come in tired and disinterested after lunch. This in itself would not have been so bad, but I had Jim Bailey in my class, one of the brightest freshmen in the school. And Jim sat there in the front row with such a look of pain on his face and with such disdain at my inability to keep Marty Shuster from disrupting things that I left school every day feeling as if I were an abject failure, a discredit to my profession.

I talked to Marty after school, suggesting that he needed to work harder and stop fooling around so much.

"You don't know me," he said. "What if my parents beat me? What if I was an orphan? What if I was dying of some awful disease? Wouldn't that make school and studying meaningless?"

"Have any of those things happened to you?" I asked.

"No, but they *could* have! How do you know they haven't?"

"You just told me," I said.

"I mean, if I hadn't told you?"

"I'd ask."

"But you don't ask everyone if they've been beaten or abandoned or if they are dying, you just assume they're okay. You just assume that they are essentially like everyone else. But they're not. Everybody's different. So how can I know you aren't assuming other false things?"

"Good question," I said. "You can't. People assume incorrect things all the time."

"So, you see, why should I listen to you at all?" he concluded. "You just might be assuming all the wrong things."

And this impasse left us staring at one another, no closer to any agreement.

"Well, I *do* know some things you don't," I insisted. "I know the assumptions most people make. I know the rules and the conventions."

"In other words, you know how to be a phoney," he replied.

I thought about that one for a while.

"Learning the conventions doesn't have to make you a phoney; you have to know them so you can participate in the culture. You have to know them in order to become *real*."

He looked up at me when I said this, skepticism etched into his brow. "Can I go to the bathroom?" he asked. "I suddenly got this royal pain in the ass."

I told Brother Blake about my problems with my afternoon class.

"Sounds like Marty isn't your problem," he said. "Bailey is. He wants you to protect him from Marty, to be his mother, but now is the time he should start to take on some responsibilities. Instead of blaming *you* for Marty's behavior, he's going to have to fashion his own response to him."

The next day, Brother Blake stopped by my class and sat in the back of the room. We were talking about *Lord of the Flies*, and I asked why, if Piggy was the smartest, wasn't he the leader? And how might civilized Ralph and his friends take over the island leadership from savage Jack and his hunters.

Jim found these questions fascinating, but no sooner had I asked them than Marty started kicking the back of Albert's chair. Brother Blake noted Jim's disgust and anger and so walked over to his desk.

"Do these students *bother you?*" he asked, pointing at Marty and company.

"They sure do," Jim replied. "They act like babies every day, and Mr. Inchausti just lets them get away with it. He tells them to stop, but they don't. He sends them outside, but they just fool around more. I'm getting sick of it."

Brother Blake ignored Marty and concentrated on Jim. "You can't always depend upon teachers and others to protect you. You're reading *Lord of the Flies*. What does it teach you about leadership? There are going to be goof-offs and troublemakers wherever you go, and the sooner you learn how to accept them, deal with them, and get on with your business, the better off you are going to be."

The class was surprised. This was the first time anyone had lectured Jim Bailey about his behavior, and yet Brother Blake had done it in a way that had put down the class rowdies at the same time. To me, he seemed to be letting Marty off the hook. That is, until I looked over at Marty and found him listening intently to what Brother Blake was saying. It was clear he hadn't ever quite looked at himself in this way.

Jim, for his part, responded with indignation. "Nobody is going to tell me I'm responsible for these loudmouths!"

"No, you're not responsible for them. But you will have to learn how to live with them. And the sooner the better. Think of Ralph on the island in *Lord of the Flies*. Without the adults there to protect him, he wasn't able to take leadership away from Jack. He was the only one there who could communicate with Simon and Piggy and make their gifts useful to the group, but he wasn't able to put Jack in his place, so he wasn't able to lead."

Jim thought this one over. "So you're saying I'm like Ralph."

"You *are* Ralph. And you'll never get off the island if you just sit around waiting for some adult to rescue you. I know it's hard.

Barbarians like Jack are everywhere. But that is what it means to go on your quest."

These last remarks, even though they were addressed to Jim, challenged Marty. Marty had always thought that *he* was the one on the quest, that *he* was the adventurer, the brave soul, the one who dared to be different. But seen through the eyes of the text and through the eyes of Brother Blake, he wasn't the hero after all. He was Jack—self-absorbed, self-centered, brutal Jack. And Jim Bailey, Mr. Goody-Goody, *he* was the hero.

Then Brother Blake walked up to the blackboard. He drew two dots and marked one A and the other B. Turning to Jim, he asked, "How do you get from A to B?"

"You draw a line," Jim replied.

Blake tossed him the chalk. "Show me."

Jim walked up to the board and drew a straight line from A to B.

A————————B

"Wrong," said Brother Blake. "The way you get from A to B is like this." And, taking the chalk, he drew a furious array of scribbles across the board.

"Now, why did I do that?" he asked the class. "Marty, you explain it to them."

Marty was surprised to find himself back in the conversation. He didn't know what Brother Blake was getting at. "You're crazy," he muttered.

But Jim Bailey, seeing Marty reject Brother Blake's example, decided that there probably was something to it.

"Are you trying to say that people don't really move in straight lines? That they have to mess up sometimes?"

"What do you think?"

"Well, I guess that's true sometimes. But you can't make a policy of messing up. I mean, you shouldn't plan to mess up; that's crazy."

Brother Blake took full measure of Jim's comment and then said, "Sometimes, the trip from A to B isn't as easy as it seems. Sometimes, it's a circuitous route, a trip up the Congo River. And you're right; you don't *plan* to mess up. It just happens sometimes. But messing up is not a bad thing if you learn from it."

Then Blake drew a whole array of possibilities.

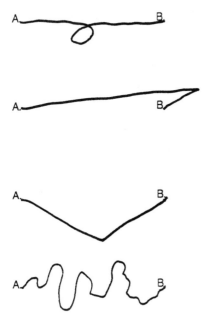

"All of these ways are valid," Blake said. "All of these ways work."

And then he had them open their Bibles to the parable of the prodigal son.

"Here is the story of a classic screw-up," he said. "The story of a guy who took the long way home. Marty, could you read it to us?"

As any master teacher might have done, Brother Blake had turned the class's attention away from the petty problem of "good behavior" to the issues raised by the texts that we were studying. But he did it in such a way that the realities of the classroom became the content of the lesson and we, ourselves, the principal subjects of the literature. My honor student's resentment was distracting us as much as his classmates' lack of discipline. And my tradition-bound views of teacherly authority were making it impossible for me to read the situation as the living embodiment of one of the themes of our reading.

I could not deny that Brother Blake's lesson had touched me—touched me more deeply than any of the lectures I had heard in graduate school. All I could do was stare at those diagrams on the board as if they were the charts of my life.

"Some of these kids," Blake told me, "think that if they aren't successful in the eyes of the world then they aren't worth anything. They believe that only the talented tenth need discipline, that the average person can float along—indeed, *should* float along—that meaningful work and the respect that it brings belong only to the few. So they seek distraction with a vengeance, as if it were their calling—their only compensation for not being superior students.

"We've got to let them know that there is another life, an inner life, a higher life, that has its own heroic dimensions. And that success in this realm is open to anybody."

Brother Blake's impact on the students was profound: here was somebody talking to them about the injustices of the school yard, the presence of bullies, the impotent "superiority" of "smart kids," and the fallibility of their teachers. Somehow, all this became more than just material for class discussions but probes that illuminated the books they were reading. Suddenly, no question seemed out-of-bounds. Everything mattered because there was no place the mind could not go. And the mind mattered because it revealed a way to act.

If anyone spoke out of turn or "messed up," Brother Blake would simply ask, "Does the prodigal son ever talk out of turn? Does his brother?"

Ideas were everywhere and in all things. The key to seeing them was in the quality of attention one paid to one's mistakes, to one's problems, to one's inevitable "messing up."

Brother Blake's lesson brought to mind thoughts of other incorrigible underground souls I had known.

When I was a senior in high school, I was a member of the Key Club, a junior Kiwanis made up largely of kids too inept to be members of any other school organization. We held meetings once a month—the last Thursday night. We didn't do much but drink sodas from McDonald's and plot how to get free lunches from our faculty sponsor. At one of our meetings, none of our officers, the popular kids, showed up. So as a joke we decided to begin impeachment proceedings against them. We thought it would be extremely funny to kick them out of office, since we knew that the only reason they condescended to be in the same club with us was to pad their college application forms.

When we began the procedures, however, Dave Deacon—a bit of an outcast—objected with surprising vehemence, raising his hand and shouting, "Point of order! Point of order!" over and over again. We ignored him and passed motion after motion kicking the officers out of the club, banning them from Kiwanis luncheons and demanding public apologies for their poor leadership.

As we proceeded, Dave got madder and madder. And the madder he got, the more contemptuous of him we got. Couldn't this "dufus" get the joke? Why was he so serious about the stupid Key Club? Didn't he know that the guys he was defending all thought he was worthless? Couldn't he see it was all a hype anyway, that our president only wanted something to add to his résumé, and that for the rest of the members, the Key Club was just a cover for parties and free lunches?

But the more cynically we abused him, the more self-righteous he became, until at last he commanded the floor—standing up on the seat of his desk with his blue parka unzipped and his geeky plaid shirt tail out.

"You know what you guys are?" he shouted. "You guys are a bunch of, a bunch of, a bunch of . . ." And it was obvious he didn't know *what* we were. He had no word for the revulsion in his heart, and he kept stuttering and repeating that last phrase until the words finally came: "You guys are a bunch of, bunch of, a bunch of ASS-BUTTS!"

There was silence in the room. No one could have imagined a more ridiculous end to his dramatic diatribe. It was too good to be true.

Finally a lone inquisitive voice broke the silence and asked, "Ass-butts? Ass-butts? Where did you get *that* word?"

The room exploded with jeering laughter. People were falling out of their chairs and holding their sides in mock pain. Whenever the hysterics would begin to die down, someone would utter that word again, "ass-butts," and all fifteen of us would be on the floor, holding our sides again, and laughing until we cried.

At first, Dave didn't laugh. He turned red, tried to make light of his mistake. "Or whatever," he said. But it was too late. For the rest of the year, maybe for the rest of his life, he had acquired a cruel new nickname.

A few years later, I was working at the college bookstore, and as I was walking across campus, I suddenly realized we were experiencing a freak snow flurry. It snows in Sacramento, California, maybe once every twenty years. Being young and high spirited, I decided that the best way to commemorate this event was to make a snowball and throw it at one of my friends. So I padded up snow in my hands and looked around for a suitable victim, when whom should I see walking across campus but Dave Deacon.

I had not seen him in three years, and yet here he was at the very moment I was seeking someone to tease. It was as if God had put him there precisely to be humiliated one more time. I hate to admit it, but the irony was irresistible to me, so I hunted him down, creeping up behind some trees to ambush him at the corner of the walk. When I got close enough to hit him, I called out, "Hey, Dave, look out for snowballs!"

He looked up—saw what I was about to do—and the whites of his eyes got large. He knew that if I hit him, the story would somehow get back to all our former classmates, maybe at some future class reunion, and he was determined not to be humiliated again. And so he did something I did not expect: He dropped his books and charged at me with the intensity of several years' worth of resentment and hatred. A raging bull, he leaped upon me, knocking me down and began pummeling me with his cold, wet fists.

"Dave!" I said. "Calm down. It was just a joke!"

But it was no joke to him. And he would take no more from me. He bloodied my lip and punched me until he cried, and then, getting up, he threw a handful of snow on my prone body, saying in utter disgust, "Tell your so-called friends James and Freddy that I beat the crap out of you." And then he walked away with more dignity than I ever imagined he possessed.

Yet, his mentioning of James and Freddy gave him away. He still craved their approval but he was convinced that he would never get it, and so he had built a citadel of scorn to hide his pain. And as I sat there in the snow, all wet, I felt for the first time in my young life abject sorrow for the person I had been and had become. If I could have taken back that snowball, I would have. If I could have erased "ass-butts" from our teenage lexicon, I would have. But I just sat there in that damn snow, bleeding, wishing I would bleed more.

In my night school course (I moonlighted like all the rest of the lay teachers), I had another frustrated "prodigal" who sat in the back of my otherwise very animated and happy English composition class. I could see all the signs of teenage resentment and seething rebellion so common at the high school.

One day, she asked if she could speak with me privately in my office. I didn't like it, but I figured I had to agree. As we walked across the campus, I asked her what she wanted, but she said she preferred to wait until we were alone before she told me. This made me even more uneasy.

We rode the elevator up to the sixth floor without speaking, and when we finally got in my office, she blurted out: "I just wanted to tell you that you are the most condescending person I have ever met in my life. I can't stand your class!"

Although I had many faults as a teacher, no one had ever accused me of condescension before—being too liberal, yes; being too forgiving, yes; suffering fools too gladly, yes; but condescending? Never! So I probed a bit to see if I wasn't the victim here of some grand Jungian shadow projection.

"Do the other students share your feelings?" I asked.

"Those sheep?" she asked. "They don't know anything!" And then she added, as if to clarify things, "I'm an art major."

Her arrogance relaxed me. She felt better just having insulted me, and I felt better knowing that she was self-aggrandizing. It made her criticisms easier to bear. A true underground figure, she felt most moral when she was lashing out. I had to refuse the shame she had thrust upon me, and at the same time, if I could do it, bring her up into the light by giving her a less vicious tool for self-expression.

I was a young enough teacher then to think I could win her back. So I took her insults as if they were observations and tried to practice teacherly satyagraha—Gandhian truth force.

But it didn't work. She continued to refuse to speak up in class or to join in dialogue with the others. She sat in the corner and smirked—continuing to get Cs on her papers and interpreting these grades as indicating her teacher's inability to grasp her secret greatness. She even fainted one day in class—apologizing profusely, saying how sorry she was to put me in such an uncomfortable position, since I obviously could not handle someone so intense, so unconventional as she.

It was hard for me not to hate her when she did these things, but I kept my pledge to acknowledge the underground, to keep the door open that led out of that psychological hell, to include her in our classroom world.

But I was never able to find the path.

It wasn't until Brother Blake had shown me the way from A to B that I began to see how a teacher might provide avenues out of the underground for his prodigal students. For some, the teacher must become the scapegoat—and stand unmoved at the center of their anxiety and contempt. This was not to say that one embraced martyrdom, but one did make it a point to stand outside the students' economy of affection as an independent standard and refuge. In this way, one became both a source of solace for a student like Dave and a contradiction to those who saw themselves as popular and protected.

Blake told me of the time a student had called him a name referring to the female genitalia in front of the rest of his students. Blake responded to this "outrage" by telling the boy not to use words he did not understand.

When the boy announced defiantly, "I know what it *means*!" Blake tossed him a piece of chalk and said, "Okay, then draw one for us on the board."

The class immediately came to attention. The other students were fascinated. Did Joe really know what one looked like? Could he draw one on the board? Would Brother Blake let him do it?

Joe walked up to the blackboard, and after a moment of hesitation, he scribbled for what seemed like a long time. When he returned to his desk, there was a smudge on the board, an oblong dot. The class of pubescent boys was mystified. Was this an accurate drawing?

Blake walked up to the picture, tilted his head to the left and then to the right. "You know," he finally said, "I have been celibate for over forty years, and even I can draw a better one than that!" The class exploded with laughter, and even Joe joined in. His anger was gone and the power of his obscenity defused by the humor.

But if Brother Blake had managed to expose the powerlessness of dirty words before the mind alive, there was one more step to be taken. The dirty words themselves had to be transformed into agents of healing.

Blake walked over to Joe, put his arm around his shoulder, and said, "You've really got to get your shit together, and to do that you need a good asshole. I am going to be your asshole this year. And after me, if you are lucky, you'll meet another asshole and another until your shit is packed so tight it coalesces into a fine powder. And then maybe you will be ready for the greatest asshole of them all."

And with that, Brother Blake stood back and pointed to the crucifix hanging above the blackboard just below the American flag.

The class gasped. It was at once the most sacrilegious and yet mystic moment many of them had ever experienced. If Jesus was the greatest asshole, then maybe they had misunderstood everything about him. What did it mean to be an asshole, anyway?

Brother Blake's image had unleashed a moment of authentic teenage reflection and religious awe. This was not sixth grade catechism, with its platitudes and trite moralisms. This was something that pulled away from schoolrooms and lesson books toward something larger and more profound. Was there nothing so secular that it could not be made sacred? No life so lost that it could not be found?

It was hard to explain to my wife, Linda, what I was going through—the lessons I was learning, and why I was so tense all the time.

The first time my wife met Marty Shuster—we ran into him at the mall—she was amazed. "So that is the kid you've been complaining about, that little four-foot-tall person?"

"Yes!" I insisted. "You don't know him like I do. Size is a relative thing."

But she was unconvinced. She was positive I was overreacting, taking my work far too seriously.

"Relax," she'd say, as if one could will emotional ease. "Don't think about teaching all the time. It's making you a very demented, even boring, person."

She was kind enough not to mention that I was also getting out of shape—gaining weight and acquiring a string of anxiety-related physical afflictions (facial tics, rapid pulse). But I couldn't help it. I had not chosen this fate; it had befallen me. Linda couldn't comprehend my stress. She just knew I was a preoccupied mess who stayed up until three A.M. every night writing and then rewriting chapters of my never-ending dissertation and spending every other waking moment fretting about Strapp, Marlowe Lakes, and Marty Shuster.

When I tried to take an interest in her concerns, she could see it was forced. I just trusted to providence that the lessons I was learning at St. Vincent's would someday pay off at home, that learning to be a teacher in the Brother Blake mold would redeem me as a husband. No, more than that, I trusted it would redeem me as a person.

But I hadn't arrived there yet, and it would strike me from time to time that Linda was wasted on me, that she had unknowingly married some yogic adept who spent far too much time contemplating classroom esoterica. Not that we didn't have our moments that first year; it was just that this teaching job loomed large in my life—perhaps too large.

There are teachers who, in order to survive, become "characters," large dramatic types—Falstaffs and Willard Scotts. For them, being a teacher is playing a role. Their personalities have big handles that the kids can hang on to. And it works!

But these same teachers become hard to live with outside of the classroom. Their family lives suffer. They don't quite fit into "normal" life anymore. It's as if becoming a teacher for them was becoming a performer, and life offstage lacks something. They aren't recognized at home, no one listens, no one has to, and so the gift of a big, easy-to-see self just isn't appreciated. In fact, its often downright annoying.

This wasn't my problem. I didn't come home from teaching an inflated personality; I came home distracted and preoccupied. Inward. Confused. I felt as though I was fighting for my life, and so I couldn't leave my worries at work. It seemed to me that each moment I forgot about my classes weakened me. I was at war, and Linda didn't really understand why I felt as though my identity was on the line with this job.

If I could become a teacher, I thought, if I could conquer this classroom of ninth grade boys, then and only then would I be *somebody*. I know it sounds silly and overblown, but that was how I felt, and I sensed that I had a chance to make it if I could follow Brother Blake. I had found something exceptional here, a real teacher, a way out.

It was the first year of our marriage, though, and Linda was working through her own problems of self-redefinition. She couldn't tell if it was our marriage or my job that had made me so distant. Was it her, or was it me? Was she finally seeing me for who I really was—a distracted, dejected, disenfranchised man?

She'd want to go to the movies, out to dinner, dance, have fun, and I preferred saving my life, meditating on my fate, replaying over and over in my mind's eye some trivial conversation I had had with Marlowe Lakes, searching for some edge or angle on the whole thing.

But I would do things with her anyway, halfheartedly, with forced attention—and then I'd stay up late after she had gone to bed, charting my next moves against the enemy, making lists and plans, revising my lessons.

Finally, we had a fight. I came home from work, and the door was locked. I couldn't get in. I knocked, knocked again, the latch turned, the door opened a peek, but the chain held fast. "Go away," she said simply. "I don't want you here."

"Come on," I pleaded. "Open the door, we have to talk."

But when the door finally flung open, I realized that I had nothing to say. I hadn't even been thinking about Linda. My mind was still back in school, on Brother Blake, on discipline problems, on Strapp.

"Well?" she asked.

I stammered. I tried to remember if I had done something or had forgotten to do something, but all I could conjure up were anticipations of tomorrow's lessons.

"You're hopeless," she finally said and walked out the door. I ran after her. "Stop! Come back! Let's talk! This is important!"

She just ignored me. She could tell it was all fake, that I just wanted to think about my class, that I was preoccupied with myself.

A few hours later she came back, although we had said nothing to lessen the tensions. She had just decided to forgive me. No, she had decided to wait for me. There would be a zone in her psyche kept in reserve, a place I could return to if I remembered where it was and if I didn't stay away too long.

I resolved not to forget.

Brother Blake's senior religion class was reading *The Little Flowers of St. Francis*, the medieval compendium of legends and accounts of the great saint's life.

"It's *Don Quixote*," he told me. "Father Mateo is Sancho Panza, and St. Francis is Quixote. It is one of the first novels, one of the first examinations of the power of a dead mythology to revivify. The kids don't see this because they don't know *Quixote*, but they see the comedy, the farce, the exaggeration, the grotesques. They see the wonderful juxtaposition of the uncomprehending prudent followers of the saint and his outrageous assertion of transcendent ideals. They see the image of a man of passion living a myth larger than life will allow.

"And the sermon to the birds is very moving to them. Francis tells the birds to be happy because they are gifted. They have wings. It's as if he is speaking to our students. Some of us think of them as animals from time to time, but never *birds*!

"I once heard the comedian Jay Leno say that talking to a fourteen-year-old boy was like trying to have a conversation with a chicken. Not only don't they listen, but they even move their necks and arms around! That was as close as I have heard anyone get to the Franciscan concept!

"Well, in the speech, Francis tells the birds to give thanks to God for the freedom of flight, beautiful plumage, and food without labor. He praises their variety and their affection, then makes the sign of the cross over them, and they rise in four separate groups,

6

Ceremonies Sacred and Profane

All I wanted to tell people was, "Honestly look at yourselves. Look at what bad boring lives you lead." That's the most important thing for people to understand. And when they do understand it, they will certainly create a new and better life. . . . Man will become better when we have shown him to himself as he is.

Anton Chekhov

December

Brother Blake's approach to teaching was changing the way I saw things. I wasn't able to teach like him yet, but I was no longer able to teach like anyone else. I was between sanities. I had lost my conventional points of reference, but I had not yet found anything concrete to replace them. To me, Brother Blake's approach was still anchored in the air.

We had a funeral on campus. Brother Bob, the crotchety, white-haired man who ran the ball room and the lost and found, had died in his sleep.

They held the service in the gym, his casket set in the center of the basketball court, a large screen propped up behind him, and a small podium where Brother Blake was to deliver the eulogy. Brother Bob's relatives sat on folding chairs about ten feet away from the casket. A woman in her forties, dressed in black, was crying modestly, but uncontrollably.

My class entered from the rear of the building—happy to have been let out of school for *any* reason.

Strapp had lectured the boys earlier over the intercom system as to the seriousness of this ceremony and the repercussions if any one of them took advantage of the situation to "make a fool of himself." Marty Shuster, however, was willing to take that risk. He saw the whole event as a once-in-a-lifetime chance to be truly outrageous. When he saw the grieving woman, he turned to his friends and mocked, "Boo-hoo! Boo-hoo!"

I couldn't tell if he was just unspeakably cruel or if this was his way of dealing with his own anxieties about death.

For my part, I found it difficult imagining Brother Bob dead. Death still seemed to me a nothing, a cipher, a mere hole in life. But there was the casket before me, the liturgy beginning to be performed, and these awful kids finding it next to impossible to keep their hands off one another.

Strapp came over and stood by my class. He wanted to make sure nothing ruined the mass.

I could not for the life of me understand why *any*one would want to hold a funeral at a high school.

Brother Charlie began to show slides of Bob's earlier years. It turned out Bob had been a fighter pilot in World War II, that he had once had jet black hair and worn a leather jacket, that he had joined the Brothers relatively late in life, that he had a younger sister who was once quite beautiful. (That was probably she, sitting in the front row.)

The slides were projected onto the large screen by one of those machines that can fade one image into the next, and as Brother Blake read the captions, we looked on in amazement at the images of a life and a world now gone.

A high school graduation portrait of Bob that resembled Terry McCloskey.

An air force flight school group photo with Brother Bob's head circled in red.

A portrait of Brother Bob as a child, dressed in a sailor suit, looking frail, hopeful, a little scared. His father, no doubt dust now, stood behind him, full of energy, powerful, strong. And beside him, Bob's mother in a floral print, her eyes sensual.

It seemed so odd. These images had more life in them than Brother Bob ever had working in that stupid ball room, passing out sports equipment. Who would have known he had had a life, that beautiful memories and a glorious history resided in the mind of that frail, if sometimes witty, old man.

My students watched the whole thing as if it were an amateur television show. They were keyed to the emotions of the event— looking to see how Strapp was reacting to things, looking to see if any of the brothers would cry. They were fascinated by adult emotions, as if they held some clue to our weaknesses.

A few of the boys tried to make fart noises without being caught; others tried to be respectful. Both were equally difficult for them— and both reactions equally phoney. I tried to note the most able actors.

Brother Blake led us in a prayer and then communion. Marlowe Lakes went down to taste the wine and returned to his seat laughing self-consciously, letting his friends know that he had participated in the mass for the cheap wine high.

Marty Shuster was still fascinated by the grieving woman. He thought she was funny.

"Where did they get those people? Central casting? Did you see that lady?" he kept asking in astonished tones. "Boo-hoo! Boo-hoo!" And then he'd giggle uncontrollably.

As we left the gym, under the tight security of Strapp's gaze, we were handed holy cards with Brother Bob's name and dates on them. Some of the kids kept theirs, others tossed them unceremoniously onto the ground, while still others waited until lunch to sketch on them. Later, I found one card with a bubble drawn just above the Virgin Mary's head with the caption, "I got Bob, now I'm coming after you!"

Brother Blake came up to me. "Your class handled this very well. Some even took communion." I listened hard to detect any irony in his voice, but I didn't hear any. What was he getting at?

At the faculty Christmas party, our secretary, Mrs. Gray, drank a little too much Christian Brothers' brandy and began to cry. It turned out she was scheduled for a difficult operation in February, and she was afraid that she was going to die.

Brother Blake listened attentively to her confession of fears and remorse, of her desire to see her son grow up, of her anger that she was being cheated by life. I got the sense that they must have been old friends when he cupped his hands as if he were catching water from a faucet and told her, "When you die, you fall into the hands of God."

"Oh, please, Blake," she protested. "Don't give me that! I'm too young. I can't leave my babies yet."

Blake looked at her closely. "But it's true. I'm not trying to comfort you."

Mrs. Gray started to sob, "Oh, Blake, what am I to *do*? What *am* I to do?"

"What *can* you do?" he asked. "I'm not too far from that door myself, but at my age, it is often a consolation to know it is there. For you, there is only faith."

"That's what scares me, Brother," she said. "I don't know if I believe."

"Well, God's there in any case," he said. "It doesn't really matter if you understand it or not, does it? Reality is reality. Death is death. Eternity is eternity. And we are all going there eventually. I'm not trying to make you feel good, Doreen; I just want to remind you that death is not the end of everything. God will still exist, and everything you knew of Him—your love, the people you loved— all *that* will remain. The stars, the sky, earth. All I'm trying to say, Doreen, is that you *can* die, and it won't *kill* you. There are worse things that can happen."

At this, Mrs. Gray laughed, then noticed me standing there for the first time, blushed, and walked away.

Had I been rude?

The Advent assembly was run by the junior class, and their adviser, Dave Rockman, intended to make the event a species of cutting-edge liturgy. The students were picking the readings and the music. Inspired by their etymological dictionaries, they had come up with the theme of *advent*ure. The adventure of Advent— *ad venire*, to come toward, to venture into reality, to journey to God.

"The plan," Dave explained to me, "is to play 'Born to Be Wild' by Steppenwolf as the students enter the gymnasium to symbolize the fact that we are all born as wild animals. The students come to school that way, and most even graduate that way. But the saving grace of Christ remains at the end of their adventure—that's the theme!

"Then right after the liturgy of the word, we play an original piece of music (composed by Jimmy McDermott) for oboe and drums. It represents the chaos of unredeemed experience."

"Sounds great," I said, unconvinced.

"And you should hear the readings the kids picked!" Dave continued. "Unbelievable! A passage from Song of Songs for the sexual adventure. Luke's account of the beheading of John the Baptist for the adventure into violence. And then the account of Jesus' assault upon the money changers for the adventure into history.

"These kids like it straight," he added. "They even suggested we have a human sacrifice, but I had to tell them that's already programmed into the mass."

"You make it sound so *pagan*," I said.

Dave glowed. "Yeah. These kids *are* pagans, primitives. It's not surprising that their liturgies resemble those pastiche assemblage ceremonies some of the New World missionaries put together with the Iroquois. This is *basic* stuff. Primal energies."

Despite his good intentions, the assembly itself was a disaster.

"What has any of *this* to do with Advent?" asked Strapp, who always stood by my class during assemblies.

"It's the Advent adventure," I replied.

"The *what*?"

We drop everything when the bell rings and march down to the gymnasium for the basketball rally.

Tonight, we are going against our crosstown rivals, the Jesuits. We beat them every year. They are the elite school—more expensive than St. Vincent's, smaller student body, more intellectual curriculum, higher Scholastic Aptitude Tests, more prestigious college admissions, two former graduates on the state supreme court. But they are sissies when it comes to sports.

We are the Christian Brothers school, private but with our roots in egalitarianism. Our graduates enter the police force, take over family businesses, or get jobs as analysts with the state government.

The students are excited today because THE CHEER-LEADERS are going to be at the rally. The cheerleaders are from our sister school, St. Theresa's. The boys tell me they are hoping to look up their skirts, watch them do splits and cartwheels, fantasize!

When we get to the gym, THE CHEERLEADERS are huddled together in the far corner of the building. Their adviser stands next to them, to serve and protect. The girls peer out at the crowd from time to time, fearfully and yet expectantly, as if somebody "important" is coming to watch them. A talent scout, maybe?

Brother Charlie nudges my arm. "Are you ready for the $3,000 pyramid?" he asks.

"What do you mean?"

"We sent the girls to cheerleader camp last summer. It cost us almost $500 per girl. When they came back, they were able to form a six-girl pyramid."

The principal takes the microphone in his hand like a lounge singer and shouts: "Christian Brothers High! Are we gonna win tonight?"

There are scattered shouts, a little applause. A disappointing rally opener.

So Brother Nep declaims, "Get it up, men!"

The boys cheer!

I wonder if he knows what he is saying and sadly conclude that he does. He then launches into one of his long-winded orations: one third theological jargon, one third educationalese, and one third misapplied teenage slang. I stand guard over my class, dying inside.

"Well, are we gonna get it up tonight or what?" (More cheers.)

"At St. Vincent's, each boy is an individual, a unique creation of God, but on the basketball court, those unique creations form a community, a team, an instrument of one single will. And we are here today to confirm that commitment, to lend the team our support, to let them know our solidarity with them is absolute!"

The students cheer, as if this made sense.

"Basketball is only one part of community life, Gentlemen," he intones. "But it is an important part, because it symbolizes our greater engagement with the struggles of life and our dedication to fair play, discipline, and the love of Christ."

Nep is getting oiled up, but he is going on too long. The students are getting antsy for THE CHEERLEADERS. He senses their impatience, cuts his speech short, and brings out the girls.

Close to a thousand teenage boys crane their necks in hope of catching a glimpse of underwear. The girls, for their part, try to make the best of an awkward situation. They keep their minds on executing the perfect six-girl pyramid and to proving to Strapp and Nep that the money they spent on cheerleader camp had not been wasted. Tracy, Cindy, Patty, Shelly, Debbie, and Brandy are models of concentration.

After dancing around a bit to the pep band's energetic version of "When the Saints Go Marchin' In," three girls hit the mat to form the base of the human pyramid. A second wave jumps upon them, and then the final girl bolts to the top and hangs on. The pyramid is up for maybe a second and then tumbles down in a massive crash.

Cheers ring through the auditorium! The girls bounce out of the hall, none of them seriously hurt (only one bloody lip).

Brother Nep takes the microphone. "Let's hear it for the girls from St. Theresa's!" And the applause rings for three solid minutes.

Outside in the hall, Strapp is organizing the girls for their escape from the school, thanking them and assuring them they had performed wonderfully. In the gym, the senior class performs several skits making fun of the Jesuits. Several students lip-synch to the Village People's recording "Macho Man," wearing little signs that read "Jesuit Student #1" and "Jesuit Student #2."

I tried to see this as good-natured fun, but it just seemed tainted to me. There were dark forces at work here. Every member of the basketball team was wearing a red sweat shirt in occult solidarity. The unexceptional others, the masses, the crowd, chanted their praise and envy. And the principal and the coaches stood there orchestrating it all like some big fascist celebration of the warrior *geist*.

How could Brother Blake accept this? He never made a peep. I saw him standing there with his class, just watching everything, turning his head now and then to take it all in. Holy Mary, Mother of God, Most Merciful Star of the Sea! Where was the Goddess energy to temper all this bogus, macho, self-regard? Where was our sister of sorrows? Where was our adoration of her mysteries?

I was so upset by the rally that, the next day, I asked my class about their attitudes toward women.

"What do you mean?" they replied. "We like 'em."

"But what do you like about them?" I asked. "What qualities make up an admirable woman?"

To help the discussion, I offered to put their list of traits up on the board.

"Good teeth!" suggested Marty.

But I insisted they get serious, and they did, providing a long litany of "more important" body parts. After they were done, I decided to speak to them straight, man-to-man.

"I'm quite a bit older than you," I told them. "And I've had girlfriends, and now I'm married. So what I'm going to tell you comes from experience. I'm not just making this up. Based upon everything I know and everything I've ever experienced, I can honestly tell you that the qualities that make for an admirable woman are not listed up on the board. They are honesty, vision, humor, and strength of character. The very same things that make for an admirable man."

And you know what? They laughed at me!

I attended the Modern Language Association's annual convention to interview for college teaching positions.

The convention was a disturbing experience for me. Coming back into the academic world after having taught at the high school was almost as unsettling as attending Dave Rockman's Advent liturgy. For one thing, all the men there looked just like me. They all wore beards, Rockport shoes, corduroy jackets, fashionable ties. I was a cliché.

But, at the same time, I felt like I didn't belong. All the other recent graduates seemed to share an idiom, a professional jargon, indeed a collective understanding of things that precluded me and my experiences at the high school.

They all considered themselves "feminists"—even the men, even the *chauvinist* men! And they would talk in shorthand—using slogans like "always already" and terms like "logocentricism," mentioning Lacan, the controversial French psychoanalyst, in almost every other sentence.

It wasn't that I didn't understand them or that they were pompous or self-regarding or even self-deceived; these were *not* extreme people. They were incredibly sane, conventional in most ways, and very smart. And yet, they seemed focused on such a narrow band of cutting-edge thinkers that they felt exempted from thinking seriously about any of the things that mattered to me.

I tried to talk to them about the ninth grade, about Brother Blake, parables, pedagogy, even prayer. They didn't reject my enthusiasms; they just smiled at them and then gave me titles of books I should read—usually complex, weighty theoretical tomes, reconsiderations of Heidegger or post-structuralist analyses of deviant historiography.

I realized I wasn't a part of their world any longer, but I also realized it wasn't too late for me to jump back into it. I had read many of these books already. I knew quite a bit of "theory." I could subscribe to the right journals. I could learn semiotics. I could . . .

No, I couldn't. I couldn't go back.

Brother Blake had ruined me. My ninth grade backwater had chastened me. I had become too aware of the pretensions of my own profession. Its scholarship seemed faddish to me now—unreal, artificial insights brewed in the styrofoam coffee cups of conference-crowd prodigies. My only hope was to connect to a "movement" of some sort—a counter-community, a subculture, preferably one of the more radical or obscure ones. Basque studies?

But when I was honest with myself, I had to admit that I couldn't really do that either. I had become a ninth grade humanities teacher, and it was my job to bring the life of the mind to bear on the lives of fourteen-year-olds. I didn't feel misunderstood at the Modern Language Association convention so much as *over*stood—and dismissed.

And yet, had any of these scholars broken up fist fights in the past year? Had any of their lectures been interrupted by spitwads to the forehead or personal insults tossed from the back of the room?

I listened to their ideas as they read their papers, wondering what they could possibly teach me about being an educator. Or even about literature? Who were these pampered aesthetes preoccupied with *epistemological* issues? How had they come to such status in the unreal city?

There is a kind of arrogance that comes from doing impossible work. You see it in urban emergency room doctors and nurses, Third World missionaries, and inner-city cops and social workers. It is a vanity born of self-sacrifice.

As a high school teacher, I was beginning to indulge in this form of self-righteousness. I knew that I was doing important work that few others wanted to do or could do. I knew that I was alive in a way others were not, that I was in the battle, in the action on the socio-historical front. It felt glorious, especially *after* work.

But a part of me was troubled by this feeling. It smacked of a provincial desire to elevate the value of one's actions to the exact degree they didn't matter. Was this merely a psychological defense against obscurity, or was I really close to one of the sources of life? I couldn't tell if I was wasting my time on trifles or doing something important. Would I wake up one morning to find myself transformed into a gigantic insect?

respond to silent prayer in his own way, for I myself had yet to fathom the full significance of this practice beyond its status as an official school ritual. But as the year progressed, I found more and more value in "attempting the impossible."

At first, I wasn't very good at it. I would try to remember the presence of God, but I was more truly just trying to imagine it—trying even just to conceive of it. I knew that this was wrong, so during the prayers, I tried to stop thinking altogether, just stop the chatter of my mind for a few seconds like they do in meditation.

I wasn't able to do this either, so I ended up just watching my thoughts course through my mind, trying not to get caught up in any of them. If I found myself inside some idea or emotion, I would simply return my attention to my breath. After a while of doing this, I noticed the same set of concerns popping up every day: Will I be able to fill up this hour? Will I get some time to relax today? What will I do if Marty acts up? Will I remember everything I am supposed to say? What if Strapp visits my room? Is my lesson plan any good? What do I have to do next?

These same worries arose so often that I soon had them numbered, and so during prayer I could simply let them go. "Oh, there's personal preoccupation #4. No need to bother about that again." As a result, after a while I was able to bring a purity of motive to my prayers that I had never before achieved, and this brought me some profound moments of rest during those three-minute reflections.

But then, beneath those surface concerns, I found another layer of stress. During prayer time, I would suddenly remember some stupid remark I had made to Strapp a week ago, or a look of disdain on a student's face that I had seen last month but had never registered. Or I'd suddenly remember something I was supposed to have done several days ago. During one meditation, I suddenly recalled an argument I had in high school with my English teacher. It was as if my mind simply refused to attend to the reality before me, as if silence and peace were impossible to obtain.

Brother Blake assured me that thoughts and images such as these bubble up in our minds all the time. We just never slow down enough to perceive them. Their logic makes up our moods. When we first try to focus upon God in prayer, we reveal to ourselves the preoccupations of our own preconscious minds. I wasn't to try to move beyond this stage, he suggested. I was to enjoy it, learn from it, catalog my worries as the first step in liberating myself from them.

This was a wonderful time in my prayer life. Every class period began with my opening a package sent special delivery from my deep self. "Oh! I'm still thinking about that? My conversation with Linda affected me more than I thought." "Oh, look at this, a fear I thought I had conquered years ago."

Occasionally, I would grow so bored of all my thoughts, feelings, plans, and obligations that suddenly my mind would become clear and the chatter cease. This would usually happen a day or two after a difficult meditation, when letting go of some particular thought had felt tantamount to dying. The students would sometimes even have to call me back to consciousness. "Mr. Inchausti, the prayer is over. Mr. Inchausti? Are you still here? Earth to teacher, earth to teacher."

When I would emerge from one of these prayers and look at my students, their presence often struck me as miraculous, and I would listen to them with renewed interest and attention in hopes of discovering *who* they were and *how* they got there.

It took me a good three months before my quest for purity of motive got God's attention, but then suddenly—out of nowhere— there it was. There was a presence with me—listening. And with God's attention, I suddenly got bigger. I felt less trivial. The classroom became an authentic battleground. Life, the school, my quest for vocation, everything seemed to matter more.

Students often evaluate their days by whether or not their teachers are in "good" moods. At first, I took this as the typical psychological defense of blaming others for their problems, but after a few weeks of silent prayer I could see their point. Events in themselves do not dictate our responses to them. A teacher in a "good" mood simply handles stress better than one in a "bad" mood. Why not simply resolve never to be in a "bad" mood, since moods are merely the result of invidious interpretations anyway?

So I resolved not to get caught up in my own self-drama or thought stream. I tried to stay true to the memory of the presence of God and see each class as if for the first time. I don't think I could have ever remembered to do that if it wasn't for that opening prayer ritual.

As the semester progressed, I began to see more and more of my life as prayer—that is, as attempting the impossible. I experienced my teaching and my praying in almost the same way: as a quest for perfect undistracted attention to the task at hand. With each task an end in itself, a door to bliss—infinitely interesting and complex.

Silent prayer was an activity that was admittedly useless, and so you could not fail at it. It didn't produce anything. It didn't satisfy any requirements. It didn't require elaborate lesson plans, and it couldn't be graded. It simply stopped everything for a minute, punching a hole in my busy, failed day and in any myth of personal or professional progress. It was done for itself and nothing more. It was a great center of calm in my stormy day, and I began to look forward to it.

Once, I promised my class that as long as they stayed silent, there would be no lessons, no assignments, no work. "If you want to," I said, "we will spend the entire period in silent prayer. But if anyone talks, it's over."

Of course, the students tried to remain silent, but they could never do it. Someone always spoke before three minutes were up. It astonished me, but they were simply incapable of being silent for more than three minutes, even when they wanted to be. They found self-control exhausting, and they were quite happy to get back to the routine of classwork after such ventures into the "impossible."

I was beginning to see that prayer was one of the most important but least understood elements in the school's curriculum. It was nothing but silence before the mysteries of life, yet that silence opened one up to infinite intuitions. When the obsessions through which one apprehends the world are allowed to dissolve, everything is revealed in a new light.

Of all the discoveries I made that first year, the power of prayer was one of the most important to me, for it helped me to get out of my mind and attend to the world in its pure, sensuous reality. It provided me with a method that bore in on phenomena instead of carrying me away into abstract speculations. I learned to rest in the presence of things *as they were*, instead of constantly fleeing from them by "figuring them out." I learned, in other words, how to let down my defenses long enough to see through my own grandiose misperceptions. I was beginning to break out of my nineteen years of schooling to a renewed faith in my own native intelligence and its spiritual core. I was at last beginning to *see* my students, rather than merely *think* about them, and prayer was my way back to this kind of independent knowledge.

I looked back into my past to find the reason why it had taken me so long to learn this simple truth. And I had to admit that my ambitions and desires had been the reason. I had sold my soul for success in school, popularity, approval. But through it all, there had remained a part of me unconvinced by the world. And this was the part evoked by prayer, by doing nothing, by attempting the impossible, and I thanked God it was still there.

I saw now that teaching itself was *attempting the impossible*, and so it too was a form of prayer—provided one did not attach oneself to the fruits of one's labors but quietly and continually tilled the soil of teenage awareness, expecting nothing, really desiring nothing, and therefore dreading nothing. Just seeing everything and providing a space for spirit to express itself.

Prayer had taught me that, to be a teacher, one didn't need to act, nor was it enough merely to wait; one could cause things to happen by opening up a space in one's heart to register the subtle movements of the students' souls toward real change. And one could do this only if one remained unimpressed by the old forms of power—progress, ability, ambition, results—and rested in the creative, unique, never-again-to-be-obtained moment of simple awareness of that which is.

My students loved to read the *Guinness Book of World Records*. They could sit for hours, amazing each other by reading excerpts.

I tried to figure out why they were so enraptured by the longest basketball game or the tallest human. Then, it dawned on me that what my students were really looking for were concrete examples of human achievements.

What they found, however, was trivia. But this didn't bother them, because at least these were "real" accomplishments. Factual. I knew, of course, that most "real" accomplishments can't be seen, let alone measured, and occur in places of the mind of which my students were only now just beginning to become aware. Most accomplishments are hard to see, because you need imagination and competence to comprehend them. Novels and scientific breakthroughs require imagination to be seen. Most people cannot perceive the accomplishments of Einstein or even Tolstoy. But world records provide concrete, measurable, specific achievements that can be grasped by even the most literal mind. My students' interest in them testified to their longings for excellence and to the paucity of avenues through which they could find it.

I didn't try to change this. I just noticed it.

8

Teaching Social Science:
The Lost Civilization of Octopia

The deep secrecy of my being is often hidden from me by my own estimate of what I am. My idea of what I am is falsified by my admiration for what I do. And my illusions about myself are bred by contagion from the illusions of other men. . . . Perhaps, if I only realized that I don't admire what everyone seems to admire, I would really begin to live after all.

Thomas Merton, *No Man Is an Island*

January

One of the projects for the year was a simulated dig involving two teams of student archaeologists. The rules were simple: each team was to invent its own culture, describe it in a series of reports, and then build and bury artifacts representing it.* The opposing team would then dig up the artifacts, try to infer as much as they could about the lost civilization, and then present their findings in a series of reports to the class. The original descriptions of each culture were then compared to the opposing archaeologists' hypotheses and prizes awarded for the most accurate findings.

In theory, this exercise was to be a lesson in inductive logic, the scientific method, and the structure of civilizations. In practice, it

---

* The complete rules and teacher's manual for this project can be found in the kit *Dig: A Simulation of the Archaeological Reconstruction of a Vanished Civilization*, by Jerry Lipetzky, published by the INTERACT Company, Box 262, Lakeside, California 92040, 1969.

resembled the muddled quest for order so brilliantly dramatized in one of my class's favorite novels, *Lord of the Flies.*

Each boy began the project with great enthusiasm, hoping to realize his fantasy of an entirely self-created world. But each discovered that his utopia did not mesh with those of the other students, and so no one's dreams were ever realized. Instead, they confronted the problems of group decision making with all its inevitable conflicts and need for compromise.

Marlowe Lakes, for example, wanted to build a city of low-riders located somewhere near San José, California, in the year 2057. Albert Perez wanted a Catholic culture whose primary values were soccer and football. Phil O'Connor wanted to create Pornotopia, a society whose central function was to cater to the sexual fantasies of teenage boys. And so they broke up into their groups, discussed their ideas, but found it hard to agree on anything.

I would help only by setting deadlines and scheduling research periods in the library, so that they could read up on civilizations and find out what governments do and how societies organize their economies.

"I need to know the name of your civilization by the end of the period," I would say unabashedly. "I also need the first draft of your civilization's history by Friday."

The left side of the class decided to create the Octopian Civilization, an undersea world populated in the year A.D. 3333 by a crashed spaceship from the planet Hardon.

The right side of the class was going to create the Artesian Civilization, a primitive, ethnically mixed culture located near San José in the year 1,000 B.C. The inhabitants of this lost civilization wore disco clothes, rode in vehicles resembling '57 Chevys, and were destroyed in the year 700 B.C., when a race riot at a local dance set off an underground neutron bomb placed there by a group of time-traveling Ku Klux Klan members from Turlock, California.

It became clear to me that my students saw their world surrealistically. Civilization to them was a hodgepodge of images and entertainments arbitrarily organized around the most fantastic premises. It was difficult for me to get them even to recognize logical inconsistencies. They had designed beef slaughterhouses in vegetarian cities, remains of spacecraft in primitive grave sites, straw huts in supposedly high-tech civilizations. Of course, all of these things could have been explained by each group's historians, but they never were. They were left as symptoms of each group's inability to reason, to get its story straight, to link individual visions to that of the group, to make a world come together if only in their shared imagination.

This project was teaching me a lot about the way my students sorted through culture. What they noticed, what they neglected. How they saw the parts but missed the whole. How their lives were littered with cultural fragments and semiotic smudges that have value primarily as consumer items and status symbols. It was as if they saw every instant as a cinematic moment; every fact, a quiz show answer; and every past deed, an old movie.

Of course, it was my job to educate them out of all this confusion, but textbook learning was not a powerful enough countermeasure. As a well-read adult, I could help them separate the plausible from the implausible and the consistent from the inconsistent, but I wasn't really all that much help when it came time for them to envision what comprised a civilization.

We pondered together over our textbook's definition. "A civilization is any organized society which possesses a system of government, monumental architecture, and leisure activities." Fine. But was this minimalist definition really of much use to someone creating one? My students were at a loss as to why people needed to organize their lives at all. They had no inkling as to the cultural purposes of central symbols, myths, and ideals. Wasn't it all free expression?

I wanted a definition of civilization that would allow their project to become a symbiosis of civics, art, science, and philosophy. I wanted my students to see their little surreal, pretend civilizations as representations of their own psyches and, hence, microcosms of their world. I wanted them to see that, in inventing a culture, they were inventing themselves. And that many other people had done this before them, had even done it better, and that they were part of a larger pattern.

The restraints of group work led many of my students to lose interest in the project. They could not abide limits, even self-imposed ones. Nor could they grasp why such limits were important. They had no sense that a culture's myths and history gave it form and significance. They could only see such values as needless restraints to their individual projects, not as givens upon which to build. They hated working within any set of organizing principles and disputed every proposed unifying theme or idea as an assault upon their individual freedom. And yet they found that merely "free" societies, without histories, without values, without prejudices, and without unifying symbols, simply dissolved into randomness.

Albert Perez, usually a very quiet boy, became outraged when his group decided that, for their religion, their society would worship cleavage.

"You guys are nuts!" he screamed. "You're sick! For religion, you worship God, not women's bodies! Mr. Inchausti, tell these guys they're doing the assignment all wrong."

I walked over to the group of seven thirteen- and fourteen-year-old boys; they were giggling and enjoying Albert's outrage.

"What's the problem?" I asked.

"They want to worship cleavage," Albert said in disgust.

"Doesn't everybody?" quipped Stevie Chambers from behind his large, horn-rimmed glasses.

The small group shook with laughter. But Albert was getting angrier.

"Look," he said. "This is supposed to be a Catholic school. You know, Mary, Joseph, and Jesus. What is this stuff about worshipping idols? You guys are weird!"

I knew this exchange was important, for it cut to the heart of two very different perspectives on religion. There was the rationalist, social science perspective held by the other boys in Albert's group.

They saw religion as one more imaginary part of their play culture. And then there was Albert's true belief. For him, religious symbols were not fictions but realities. To detach himself from their values would constitute a betrayal. For the others, to take them seriously was to embrace the absurd. And so they stood apart from one another, separated by a psychological and logical abyss.

I wanted to point out the value of Albert's committed stand while at the same time pointing out the value of the group's scientific detachment. Religion may, in one sense, be a sociological phenomenon, but it is also an iconography of ultimate concern. The fight over "The Cleavage Cult" carried us into modern controversies over the secularization of culture, the nature of faith, and the status of the erotic in public life.

I didn't want to step too far into the group's dynamic and deny Albert his chance to be a courageous outsider defending his values against—in his mind, anyway—a corrupt majority. Nor did I want to deny his group the liberation of smashing a few icons by inventing a fictive religion around the most awesome mystery they knew: breasts.

I thought for a moment about what Strapp, the school vice principal, might think of all this and how it would look on back-to-school night if my class produced twenty cultural artifacts all deifying the human bosom. I decided, not without a little fearlessness, that it might not look at all bad. What would be wrong about amateur archaeologists digging up tiny replicas of the Venus of Wallendorf? In fact, it would reflect the perennial interest in primordial images. This imaginary "cleavage" religion might, in fact, be a more authentic expression of sacred teenage awe than the more conventional religious practices I had already approved for their Octopian counterparts.

My solution, if one could call it that, was to allow the group to proceed as it saw fit and allow Albert to write up his minority position. He could create an artifact reflecting the values of his dissenting minority, the oppressed Catholics of Artesia. And the group promised to integrate his minority views in their history and material culture. I reminded them, however, that there were school rules against the possession of pornography.

At this proviso, Stephen got a little defensive. "Look, we're not going to use porno, okay? We just worship knockers; that's our religion!"

I could tell by the tone of his voice that the Artesian culture would be no tribute to the goddesses of prehistory. At its best, it would be an unsentimental mirror of our times; at its worst, an expression of teenage sexual stupidity presented as a parody of religion. A chill ran through me as I realized that I was no match for the sophisticated corruptions of the age.

I needed to discover for myself how the fictive worlds of my students connected to their aspirations. And I needed to speak to those aspirations in a way that overcame the ridicule and sarcasm that comprised their defenses against being educated.

I didn't want this assignment to be just another school project—something they did *for* Mr. Inchausti. I wanted it to tap into some of the energy they expended at home in their backyards, inventing invisible cities with sticks and old toys. Only this time, those cities would be seen, talked about, and understood—brought into dialogue with social science, history and religion.

Was I too ambitious?

When the students finally got around to making their artifacts, the spirit of competition came into play, and so they tried to create ambiguous representations in order to throw off the analyses of the opposing team's researchers. Each team was to have at least one "Rosetta Stone" to give the other group's linguists the possibility of deciphering their language system. Both teams decided that if they had to have such a clue, they would disguise it—writing the translated terms upside down or in code—so that it would make sense only if read in a mirror.

Marlowe Lakes hid his artifact (a disco dance instruction manual) inside a bologna sandwich in the hope that it would putrefy before the opposing team's archaeologists got to it. Toy cars smashed beyond recognition were used to represent nuclear destruction, and tubes from old TVs were supposed to indicate high-tech achievements. Secret tombs were built so that they would collapse if uncovered too quickly. More attention and ingenuity went into devising ways to keep one's culture a mystery than ever went into creating the culture in the first place. What fascinated my students was deception, cunning, winning the game, and fooling their friends. I found out later that dog excrement had been used to protect the entrance to the holiest Artesian temple (a strategy, I later discovered, not without historical precedent).

At the close of the dig project, we held a mock professional conference on "lost civilizations" with students from each group delivering scholarly "papers" on their findings.

Stephen Chambers, professor of archaeology at Wottsamotta U., delivered the opening paper on the nature of religion in Civilization X, known by its inhabitants as "Octopia."

"The Octopians seem to have worshipped the dolphin," he began. "Pictures of dolphins can be found on city walls, inside books, and on the remains of buildings that resemble temples. Unlike the Artesians, whose interest in cleavage indicates a hedonistic society, the omnipresence of the Octopian dolphin suggests a people in love with the sea. Perhaps they were commercial sailors or fishermen or explorers. They probably saw dolphins every day, out ahead of their ships, glistening in the sun, moving through the water like demigods. The Octopians must have admired that. They must have wanted to be just like dolphins."

There was a scattering of applause at this impressive speech, and then the Octopian team got its chance to explain what their culture was "really" about. But before Mike Todd could offer his formal presentation, his partner Jim Nettles broke the formalities by shouting out, "You're wrong, Chambers! Way off! We don't worship dolphins! We EAT dolphins! You lost, man! The building you thought was a temple was really a cannery. Ha! Ha! Ha!"

It was a poignant moment, because Stevie had imagined a more beautiful civilization than had "really" existed. His imaginative achievement had become an error and source of personal ridicule.

Jim Nettles continued his barbaric diatribe.

"As far as religion goes, Stevie baby, we're Catholic!"

Stevie, to his credit, was not in the least impressed by this last bit of information.

"No," he said. "You may call yourselves Catholic, but if you eat dolphins, then the evidence indicates that you worship your own stomachs."

Nettles remained triumphant. "Awww, admit it, Chambers, we fooled you. You're just mad because you lost."

Stevie wasn't really mad about *that*. He was mad that the cruder vision had triumphed, that the less beautiful explanation had prevailed. He was upset that the Octopians had such a crude sensibility.

Stevie pretended to update his paper and asked to make a second presentation "in light of the new revelations."

"It won't count!" shouted Nettles.

"I know," replied Stevie. "I just want to set the record straight."

And so, with the same dignity with which he had presented his first paper, Stevie ascended the podium and gave the following address:

"One day," he said, "before your Octopian civilization existed, there was a Land of the Dolphin. A land rich in love and filled with hope for the future. They lived in harmony with nature until a crude, savage tribe of human beings called Octopians began to destroy their world. These Octopians ate them and then drew pictures and told stories about them as a record of what had been lost. And so the real religion of Octopia, its real link with God and the universe, the source of all its stories, pictures, and songs, is its memory of the free dolphin, its memory of a lost time of innocence."

It was a miraculous speech. Where had he learned such things? Where had he found the courage? It suddenly became clear to me that culture is simply a heroic stay against disillusionment, an act of bravery and will, an assertion of the sublime. And if it cannot defeat death nor overcome history nor save our souls, it can, nevertheless, do something almost as great. It can increase our energy and our wonder, making us into new beings: intense, alive, respiritualized.

For the first time, I was beginning to hear what my students had to teach me.

9

Teaching English Composition: The Spirit and the Semicolon

If, instead of saying: This drawing is wrong, incorrect, badly drawn, etc., they would say: Isn't this in bad taste? isn't it insensitive? isn't that an insentient curve with none of the delicate awareness of life in it?—But art is treated all wrong. It is treated as if it were a science, which it is not. ... Art is a form of supremely delicate awareness and atonement—meaning at-oneness, the state of being at one with the object.

D. H. Lawrence, "Making Pictures"

February

I landed a part-time job at night at the university, counseling students who had failed the university's graduation writing exam. I would meet with them one-on-one in a small conference room to explain where their writing needed improvement.

I started to thumb through the papers when I came upon the name of the daughter of one of the science teachers at St. Vincent's. I pulled her file and found that she had written only one or two sentences in her exam booklet, then crossed them out—a clear symptom of writer's block or test anxiety. My job would simply be to ease her mind.

Or so I thought.

When she came into my office, she was not really interested in getting help or reassurance; she was mad. The instant that she walked through the door, she declared, "That test question was *not* fair!"

The question read:

Each of us at one time or another has tried to teach somebody something with varying degrees of success. Perhaps you tried to teach a younger brother or sister to drive or to do long division. Or maybe you taught a coworker how to operate the machinery at your place of employment.

Describe a time you tried to teach something to somebody. Tell us the results, and then explain how you would do it differently the next time.

"It seems a fair question to me," I said.

"But you're a teacher. I've never taught *any*body *any*thing. How am I supposed to write an answer to a question about something I've never done?"

"Surely other people have taught *you* things," I said. "Can't you imagine what it was like?"

"Do you mean *make something up*?" she asked, as if I had just suggested she rob a bank.

"Yes!" I said. "Use your imagination!"

At this, she collapsed back into her seat, looked away from me for a moment, moved the lower portion of her jaw a bit as if to make room for her tongue, then looked me in the eye.

"Use your imagination? Use your imagination? USE YOUR IMAGINATION! Everybody keeps telling me to *use my imagination*! Don't you people understand: I DON'T *HAVE* AN IMAGINATION!"

I was dumbstruck. I could tell by her despair that she was probably telling me the truth. She had no imagination, and how was a $7-an-hour counselor going to fix that?

I told her that she was probably wrong about herself—that she no doubt had an imagination and the ability to invent abstractions, but it was merely translating those ideas into words where things broke down. I showed her some brainstorming strategies and talked about rhetorical invention, but she was not reassured. She listened to me halfheartedly, distracted, convinced nothing could come out of any of this.

When I had finished with all my neat techniques, she looked out at me from behind a shock of blond hair.

"Yes. Okay. I see. Can I go now?"

She was nursing a sense of self-ruin that I could not penetrate.

"Sure," I said, trying to wind things up. "It's all just a matter of asking yourself the right questions."

"No," she insisted. "Its *not* just that; you've got to be able to answer them too."

"Well, yes," I said. "But that's the easy part."

"Is it?" she asked in anger. "Is it *really*?"

"I guess it does take a little practice," I admitted, and then I suddenly felt ashamed.

I didn't know why then, but looking back on it now, I can see how glib and self-serving my advice was. She thought writers had to be honest. She had failed the exam, in part, because she believed that. And here I was, the sophist, attempting to initiate her into disingenuousness. To pass this test, she had to be more playful, less serious, even a little deceitful.

She didn't want to lie, and she didn't want to succeed in a world where insincerity was rewarded. I had tried to cure her of this childish vanity by trotting out all the dogmas of my college composition books, but I really had nothing to say to this girl. I had no way of disclosing to her the origins of originality, for if the truth be known, I was not a very original person myself. I had only formulas, a few pedagogic tricks, a grab bag of false noses and eyeglasses from which to feign eloquence. And she was asking me if, as a writer, she could live without them.

Had she been a great intellect—a world-class physicist for example—I'm sure I would not have presumed to instruct her on the art of dissimulation; but she was just a middle-class girl, a sophomore at college, and so my condescension held no bounds. Again, it was Brother Blake who offered me another way of looking at the art of composition.

When the local school district held its annual training day at Lincoln High School, Brother Blake and I were sent to represent St. Vincent's English department. The theme for the day was "Back to Basics," and after a major address by educational psychologist Peter Mead the teachers broke up into small groups organized around their respective disciplines. In these meetings, the teachers presented their curricula, traded instructional strategies, and discussed methods.

Calvin Grady, a thin man in his early forties from Lincoln High, was chair of the English teachers meeting. He was anxious to show off what he considered to be the most basic, back-to-basics English curriculum in the entire state. His impressive program had students moving progressively from short paragraphs to process essays, to comparison and contrast themes, culminating in argumentative prose. Detailed records were kept of their grammatical skills, and everything they ever wrote from the ninth grade to their senior year was kept in a file in a storeroom located beneath the cafeteria.

The paperwork alone was so massive that they had to hire a part-time teacher's aid just to handle the filing. But in the future, they hoped to store student writing in a computer. Grady passed out year-by-year instructional goals, methods, and assignments and a five-page policy statement.

"Of course," he conceded, "this program works best for our college preparatory students. Emily Monet handles the remedial students, and she can answer any question you have in that area."

Emily Monet was my age, a beginner, and I could see in her eyes the same exasperation and self-doubt I knew so well. The remedial classroom was where all the "problem" students ended up, and just getting their attention was a major accomplishment. In fact, in the middle of an unruly classroom, curriculum seemed a small matter.

I wondered if Monet had ever met anyone like Brother Blake to help her out, to reassure her that she was closer to the heart of education than her "superior," Grady, no matter how shiny and complete his college prep files. I wondered if anyone would acknowledge how important she was or address her problems as a teacher, or if all the attention and planning would be devoted to Grady's heady, impressive program.

Monet spoke briefly, almost apologetically. "In the remedial sections, we work on sentence structure, mechanics, and usage. It's pretty basic stuff, and the students have a hard time, but we do see progress." There were no questions from the audience.

I could picture the classroom in my mind: tired, bored, restless teenagers—bewildered by Monet's interest in subject-verb agreement. And I could see Monet herself, torn between the needs of her students, articulated in their tired eyes, and the ambitions of her curriculum, intent on pounding basic skills into those passive teenage skulls, even if it killed them.

The presentations ended, and all the teachers sat down, hoping that no one else would "sell" any particular program.

Brother Blake began the discussion. "Before we go on, maybe we should consider the question of what is basic?"

"Well, I think the semicolon is pretty basic," Grady said. "Don't you?"

Half the room laughed and nodded in agreement. The other half, perhaps put off a bit by the self-serving nature of Grady's previous presentation, looked curiously at Brother Blake, hoping that this strange man in the clerical collar would contradict him.

He didn't let them down.

"But surely semicolons are not basic," Brother Blake replied. "They are quite a sophisticated punctuation device not invented, in fact, until well after the Norman Conquest. Isn't language itself more basic?"

There was tension in the room now. Brother Blake had crossed the line that separated pleasant fellow professionals from troublemakers. He had asked an intellectual question that challenged a colleague's basic assumptions.

"What are you talking about?" Grady asked. "Our students know the language. What they need are writing skills—rules, conventions, guidelines."

Brother Blake did not respond immediately. Everything Grady
had said was true enough in its own fashion. Yet, it clearly wasn't
the whole story. Otherwise, why weren't the students learning to
write, why were the remedial classes so large, and why was the
hubris of bureaucratic programs so insufferable?

Thinking out loud, Brother Blake tried out an analogy. "Maybe
language is like a car. We have to teach them how to drive, where
to put in the key, and how to change a flat tire, but they won't
listen to us if they don't have anyplace to go. So we have to
consider the larger purposes of language itself and how and why
these kids use it if we want to inspire them to be effective
writers."

I immediately thought of all the metaphors for language I had
studied in graduate school. Wittgenstein's analogy of the tool box
and Nietzsche's image of the prison house. I wanted to bring them
to bear here, to show Brother Blake that these issues had been
considered before. I wanted to tell him about all the new research
taking place, that there were people who *specialized* in composition theory. But somehow, it didn't seem pertinent. Brother Blake's
hackneyed trope of the car spoke to the situation at hand more
directly and eloquently than any of the abstract theories rattling
around in my brain.

Grady responded strongly. "I don't care where they drive, so
long as they know the rules of the road. As teachers, we serve our
students' freedom, we don't guide their lives. And we serve their
freedom by providing them with the tools necessary for self-direc-
tion—such as semicolons."

"All I am saying," Brother Blake interrupted, "is that writing is
basically about *that*." And all eyes followed his finger as he pointed
to the bulletin board next to the front blackboard, on which was
pinned "Let Your Spirit Shine Through" in yellow construction-
paper letters next to a yellow construction-paper sun.

Monet was the first to break the uncomfortable silence.

"Yes, I guess spirit is most basic. But we can't teach that, now,
can we?"

"You don't have to teach it," Blake replied. "You only have to acknowledge it. And you don't acknowledge it by pouring all your energy into perfecting these gimmicks. Students have got to see that you love language, and eloquence, and metaphor—not that you're a professional who knows more than they do."

"Oh, come now, Brother Blake," Grady replied. "We're only high school teachers trying to save the semicolon from global extinction. It is a small but honest calling. God help us if we ever begin to take ourselves too seriously."

Then, Brother Blake launched into one of his famous mini-lectures.

"There are," he said, "two wills. The false will and the real will; the artist and the hack; the voice of prattle and the Universal Self. Mindfulness, of the sort experienced through reason, meditation, and prayer, activates the real will. And so before one can write, one has to wake up. In other words, one's perceptions have to be educated to a kind of Platonic turning from the world of becoming to the world of being. And even though one never arrives at being, the search for universals links one's writing to the philosophical quest.

"The attraction of process models is that they hold out the hope that technique, if refined enough, may, in fact, turn into substance. The problem with this is that it assumes that, to be a writer, no real change of heart or metanoia need occur—that our natural lives are enough, sacred in their radical secularity, lacking merely adequate expression or aesthetic acknowledgment. Seen in this way, writing becomes a substitute for and distraction from the serious work of knowing reality. A cruel hoax.

"But if writing is seen as the most literal articulation of the human quest for being, then it is *nothing but* substance."

He let this one sink in for a while.

"Look," he said, "serious writers do not know how they create. But they do know how they work. And this know-how is passed on as if it were the essence of writing itself, but it isn't. Yet, composition instructors are helpless to speak any deeper on the matter. Only the mystics can! Longinus and the Plato of *The Phaedrus*—they are the great composition theorists."

"But how can you teach this?" Grady asked. "We are talking about fourteen-year-old boys. Most of them forget to bring their pencils to class."

"I'll show you," Blake said. He pointed to a tree outside the classroom and asked, "Where is that leaf?"

"On the tree," Grady answered.

"Wrong," Blake said. "Look again."

"Okay, it's on the end of that Y-shaped branch."

"Wrong again," Blake said. "It's *in the air.*" And holding up his two fingers as if he were holding a grape floating in space, he enacted the miraculous fact that leaves are literally suspended in midair.

"And that's where ideas come from," he said. "They are in the air. Of course, when you write, you organize your papers the way God organizes a tree—you attach the idea to a branch of thought, and that branch adheres to the more solid trunk or discipline, which is rooted in the earth of our shared experience. That's what writing is all about: linking the miraculous perception to the material universe."

It was an elegant image, and it had an element of genius to it. Compositions should have shapes—like trees. And ideas could appear anywhere—like leaves—floating in the air. If you were alert, you could see them. It was a liberating idea. And you could demonstrate it Socratically!

I remembered a similar trick Brother Blake had pulled on me in the hallway. He asked me, "How do you get from that mark on the floor to that larger mark six feet away?"

"You walk," I had replied.

"No," he said. "You do this!" And then he walked over to the large mark. "You do it!" he said. "You don't *say* how it is done. That's the trouble with intellectuals—they have minds but no hands or feet. They lack the capacity or the desire to do the work their insights reveal to them must be done, so they write books on why life is impossible. You're lucky you weren't a better student. You'd probably be teaching at Harvard now, giving lectures on the necessity of walking across the street."

There was a legend that Brother Blake had once been asked by the senior class to speak at their graduation. His talk lasted exactly thirty seconds.

"Some of you," he was reported to have said, "have taken the journey to the center of your minds and have made the liberating discovery that it does not exist."

Now that I had heard his parable of the leaf, I knew what he must have meant. Consciousness does not exist inside us but persists all around us. Ideas are as numerous and as present to hand as the leaves on the trees. To think clearly, one needs to be less self-conscious, not more so. And finding your voice, as a writer, is really just finding your authority as a person. Knowing what you can say in all honesty from where you stand. Writing is, in effect, the soul seeking its context, and in finding its context, discovering itself.

When you are fourteen, what can you say with surety and conviction? Not much. But you can speak powerfully out of your innocence, out of your longing, out of your isolation. Some of the best student papers I ever received were written in that searching honesty of innocence that looks across at the adult world as if it were on the other side of a chasm—and rather than mimic the pseudosophistications of a conventional grown-up, expresses the simple, yet revolutionary observations of the newly born. Rimbaud has that voice.

I sat beside the road
That soft September night—listening.
The dew upon my face
Like strong wine.

And in the shadows, I made rhymes,
Plucking the laces of my
Wounded shoes like a lyre—
One foot pressed against my heart.*

One boy in my class wrote a beautiful account of meeting his "real" parents. He had been adopted, and he once flew back East somewhere to spend a week with them. They were, in his words, "nice people." And he described to perfection their house, their manners, their clothes, their conversation.

But then, he ended the essay with the sentence: "And then I got on the plane and returned to the people who loved me." I can still remember that line. I nearly cried; it was so perfect. He had seen through it all and affirmed his life in his own voice with the authority earned by seeing his place in the scheme of things.

What we are seeking as teachers and writers too is our place in the scheme of things—our true authority. If we assume too much, we are sentimental and bombastic. If we assume too little, we are academic and thin. But if we can grasp our context with perfect honesty—and it sometimes happens that we do—then our writing becomes the perfect expression of who we are, and as such it has to be beautiful.

Most students think writing has more to do with grammar than the search for reality. But learning to write—like learning to teach—is as much an act of courage as it is an act of linguistic skill.

I asked Brother Blake why he didn't write a book on English composition.

"I'm a teacher," he said. "I write like Jesus: with my finger in the dirt."

---

*From "My Bohemia," author's translation.

10

Teaching Social Justice:
The Classroom as Culture Clash

We cannot change the world by a new plan, project, or idea. We cannot even change other people by our convictions, stories, advice and proposals, but we can offer a space where people are encouraged to disarm themselves, lay aside their occupations and preoccupations and listen with attention and care to the voices speaking in their own center.

Henri Nouwen, *Reaching Out*

March

My successes were building, and I was gaining new confidence. I was learning as I was teaching, and I was teaching what I was learning. Each lesson seemed to be the culmination of everything I ever knew. I was not yet Lao Tzu, but I was getting closer. I was on the path.

In our unit on economics, the students were paid for everything they did, and in the end, grades were to be auctioned off to the highest bidders, and there were a limited number of passing grades.

To make this simulation more realistic, each student was symbolically born into an economic class by random draw. The economic classes matched the distribution of income in the United States. It was decided a *world* scale of distribution would be just too disheartening. As it was, the students were amazed by how many of them were born into poverty.

Our wealthy students would get extra classroom space, higher pay, limitless supplies. In fact, our super-rich student—it happened to be Marty Shuster—owned half the room and nearly all of the desks. He'd sit there in the middle of his "estate" with no other students near him, like some boy sultan, happy to have won the draw—but vaguely self-conscious and uncomfortably isolated.

The lower- and middle-class students, the vast majority, crowded their desks into the remaining area. They had to pay rent to Marty if they moved into his territory. The very poor shared broken and defective desks in the slum at the rear of the room.

The students were free to set up any kind of constitution or system of government they wished. But as you might have guessed, they modeled their city upon what they knew. Democratic elections got them a president who was quickly bought off by the richest citizens. The poor spent most of their time arguing with the police; the wealthy spent their time devising self-serving tax structures and protectionist legislation. The middle class was divided: some sought wealth, others reform, still others just enjoyed playing cop.

The less disciplined students seemed capable of generating the most enthusiasm for the least worthwhile projects, while the *serious* students found support for their reasonable reforms difficult to "sell."

I tried to get the students to reflect on the meaning of the events of our simulation in terms of social justice, public policy, and Biblical commentary. But this was difficult, because the students gave themselves over so passionately to their roles and because their class identifications were so strong.

To overcome this, I let the simulation break down from time to time and then used the resulting dysfunctions to get them to think critically about the game itself. We read Joseph Holland's essay "Humanizing the Third Stage of Industrialization," published by the Center of Concern, and I tried to explain some of the church's positions on economic reform and the role of the poor in history.

But such ideas seemed to matter less and less as the competition of the game became more intense. The students just wanted to win those damn passing grades.

Ben Brown started a newspaper in order to "expose the self-serving tax plan of our city's richest citizen."

I lent him five hundred "Room 207 Smackers" to print his first edition. It was a home-typed, photocopied affair with several *Mad Magazine*-style cartoons and a huge exposé of Jim Bailey's scheme to make Marty Shuster his partner and then take over the class economy.

But the middle-class students thought that Ben was just out to make a buck at their expense, so they refused to buy his paper.

"Guys!" he'd plead. "I'm just trying to tell you what's happening—Marty and Jim are gonna win the game. They're *gonna* take over. Read my paper. I got proof. I heard them talking at lunch. I quote them and *everything*!"

"Yeah?" said Marlowe, "then why don't you just give us the paper free?"

"Because I *need* the money!"

Two days later, Ben switched the format of his newspaper from hard news to gossip about the other students, and he began to make sales.

"They want jokes and gossip," he confided to me after class. "They love put-downs. They don't even *want* to know what Jim is up to."

I was struck by his heartfelt disappointment over what it meant to be a newspaper man.

Try as I might to put this game into some overall perspective, I found that the simulation was just too lifelike to comprehend. Analogies to actual sociopolitical realities abounded, but I was just not artful enough to understand, let alone explicate, all the emerging lessons.

The poor and the lower middle class quickly saw that they were facing a structural disadvantage built into the very rules of the game, which made it impossible for them to compete for grades. But they were at a loss as to how to change the rules without seeming to be spoilsports.

Albert Perez, who, in fact, was from a lower-middle-class family, found himself symbolically born into poverty for the simulation. At first, he protested, telling me, "I'm tired of never having enough money. Even if it's only make-believe, couldn't I be rich just this one time?"

But I stuck to the luck of the draw and did not allow him to trade economic places with anyone else.

A few weeks later, he wrote an essay on the meaning of poverty:

> When you are poor, you give up on some things but not on others. You give up on being a big shot; you know you can't show off. But you never give up on yourself. You're all you've got. And so you stay quiet, and say to yourself, "They might have more, but I know what's real."

By contrast, those students symbolically born into wealth sought ever more expansive money-making projects. They made "international" agreements with the "wealthy" students in other classes, who were playing a similar simulation, and put together a "world bank" so they could regulate the currency. (Ah! So that's what the World Bank is all about!) They even began to organize a "world" government so they could generate new markets. They resisted all attempts at altering the rules, calling them tricks to steal their money away. And they demanded—above all—that the grade-distribution rules not be changed *on ethical grounds*.

"A rule is a rule," they argued. "We can't switch now. It wouldn't be *fair!*"

Such ironies were not lost upon our poor students, some of whom tried to build a grass-roots movement to oust the president. But President Bailey reminded them that, as a former lower-middle-class person himself, he was well aware of their problems. A revolution would earn everyone Cs, he warned them, and he wanted to make sure that individual effort was rewarded.

There were also moments when the game took on a strange power to inform our literary readings with new meanings. The beatitudes, for example, when read aloud, drew cheers from the poor students. And the students symbolically born rich suddenly found the courage to question the traditional Christian pieties that they had mouthed in their catechism classes. They found many New Testament ideas about the dangers of money "unrealistic," "for another time," "not really what Jesus meant."

The day we auctioned off the grades, there were three As to be purchased, six Bs, twelve Cs, six Ds, and three Fs. According to my records, the richest student in the class was still Marty Shuster. He had accumulated approximately $2,000 in "Room 207 Smackers," primarily through his real estate transactions renting desks and selling property.

The second richest student was Jim Bailey, who had amassed around $1,000 by helping Marty collect rents and serving as Marty's "attorney" at the class constitutional convention, a convention he also presided over as class "president."

The third richest student was Marlowe Lakes. No one knew exactly how much money he had, since he had earned most of it running a lunchtime gambling casino in the school cafeteria. He had brought his brother's toy roulette wheel to school along with the green felt betting tally and a large supply of red, white, and blue plastic chips. I estimated his holdings somewhere around $750.

The rest of the students had about $450 each, except for the poor, most of whom either had nothing at all or owed a little money to Marlowe or Marty.

Marty bought the first A for $1,000.

Jim Bailey bought the second A for $1,000.

When the third A went up for bid, Marlowe offered $900. He had made more money than any of us thought.

But then Marty entered a bid of $1,000.

"Hey, wait a minute," Marlowe protested. "You already got your A. What are you going to do with another one?"

"Keep *you* from having it," Marty jeered.

And then, Jim Bailey slapped Marty on the back, and they both broke out in peals of laughter.

"This is *bull*shit," Marlowe declared. "Can he do this?"

"Well, I don't see any law against it," replied Jim. "And as class president, I think we would be infringing on Marty's rights if we blocked him from spending his money any way he wants to. This is a free country, Marlowe! Ha. Ha. Ha."

Then Stevie shouted out, "Hey, Marlowe, come here. I think we can make a deal."

Stevie and Marlowe conferred a few minutes.

Bailey protested. "Mr. Inchausti, they're holding up the game! Come on, they can't do this!"

"I don't see any law against it," mocked Marlowe. "Besides, we're done."

Then, standing up, so that he could be heard by everyone, Marlowe changed his bid. "I would now like to bid $1,500 for that A."

"You don't have that kind of money," taunted Marty.

"Well, I don't," admitted Marlowe. "But with Stevie, Teddy, and I putting our money together, we do. The STM Syndicate buys the last A."

"You can't all get A's!" pointed out Jim Bailey. "You divide an A three ways, and that's a C, baby. No better than a C. Maybe even only a C minus!"

"We don't want the crummy A, Bailey," said Marlowe. "We're giving it to Albert."

And suddenly, Albert looked up from his ghetto-zoned broken desk. He had written off the whole simulation as an exercise in futility and had resigned himself to an F. But this was an interesting development.

"Yeah," Marlowe said. "We give the A to Albert. And you "Sucks" can have the other two. As for the STM Syndicate, we want the Fs. Mr. Inchausti, could you have those Fs embossed in gold leaf? I'd like to mount mine."

"You guys are nuts," declared Marty in disgust.

"You're wrecking the game!" protested Jim.

"No, we're not wrecking the game," replied Marlowe. "We're making it *jam!*"

And then, the three members of the STM Syndicate slapped hands in a triple-high-five.

Teachers in secular institutions who use this simulation may be at a disadvantage by not possessing a shared, if disputed, religious tradition to help them mount a cultural critique of the economic system. "A man's best friend is his dogma." But that does not mean that a similar ethical criticism could not be based upon secular principles. Humanism is a dogma in its own right; so is feminism.

But it is not enough merely to possess an ethically engaged world view; one must know how to set it into operation in the classroom. This is what Brother Blake knew how to do so well. Every lesson, every discipline problem, every school event was a potential epiphany, and he had trained himself to see them that way.

The classroom, with its overt and covert resentments, with its prejudices and competitive edge, is still one of the best places to teach social justice because it is THE ZONE OF CONTEMPORARY CULTURE CLASH: the place where innocence meets experience, passion meets apathy, the present meets the past, and the past meets the future.

Blake's approach, coupled with our economic simulation, lifted everyday problems above personality conflicts into a universal realm policed by the formal disciplines: literature, philosophy, theology, and history. It gave credibility to the intellectual life as an authentic way to confront the world. And it affirmed the students' own experiences as worthy of serious reflection.

In the Old Testament, there are essentially three spiritual vocations: the priest, the prophet, and the sage. The priest interprets scripture and enacts ritual. He is the conservative force in the community of the faithful, the keeper of tradition. The prophet is the visionary, the revolutionary, the man on the cutting edge who possesses a unique perspective that throws new light on all that went before. The sage is the wise elder who brings both tradition and prophecy to bear upon the present.

As teachers in the humanities program at St. Vincent's, we were not called upon to be either priests or prophets, but we were called upon to be wise. This meant that, in our attempts to teach social justice, we were not to be divided by the clash between the authority of the past and the energy of prophecy, but to use both to throw light on the realities of the lives of our students in our classrooms. My job was not merely to be an agent of socialization or a proselytizer for some privileged ethic. I was to be there at the scene of an orchestrated culture clash to aid in the birth of creative discovery and response.

Marlowe came into class one afternoon and declared that he had changed his name to Bootsy. "From now on, Mr. Inchausti, my name is *Bootsy*. Call me Bootsy."

I said, "Come on, Marlowe, you can't change your name."

And he said, "What?" There's nobody here named Marlowe. My name is *Boot*sy."

After school, I asked Brother Blake what I should do.

"Call him Bootsy," he said.

"But the other students will think I'm giving in to him." I protested.

"Then have them read James Baldwin's essay "Nobody Knows My Name" or that section in *The Autobiography of Malcolm X* on names. Or the passage in the narrative of Frederick Douglass where he picks a new name based upon a character in a heroic novel by Sir Walter Scott. Teach them the history of names and the reasons Marlowe might very well want to change his. Ask them why Kareem Abdul Jabbar changed his name and why Muhammad Ali changed his.

"You know name changes are also a big part of the Old Testament tradition; remember Jacob's name is changed to Israel. It usually signals a radical change in a person's life. Of course, Tony Curtis and Troy Donahue changed their names too; we have *that* degraded show biz tradition to deal with. But let the kids examine it!

"You know, you could change your name too," he suddenly exclaimed, as if surprising himself. "Have them call you 'Bossman Charley' if they want. And let the rest of the kids change *their* names. You could make it a class project. Have them write essays on their names—the ones given them by their families, the ones given them by their friends, and the ones they'd choose for themselves. Let them discover on their own what's in a name."

Jimmy Hastings ran into my room.

"They shot Reagan," he said. "I just saw it on TV in Mr. Clooney's room. They got tapes of the whole thing."

Immediately, I felt nauseous and shaky.

"Is he dead?" I asked.

"No, they say he's okay, but some other guy got blown away."

"Can you see that on TV?" Marty asked.

"Not really, you can't see much, just some people ducking and then the Secret Service guys pulling out all their weapons. Its *awe*some what they carry. Man, they pull out automatics and all kinds of shit!"

I immediately thought of all the reassuring, but incorrect, reports the day Kennedy was shot, about how he was "okay," the lies about how only Connolly had been hit.

My room didn't have a television, so our only source was Jimmy.

"Can you see any blood?" asked Ben Brown.

"Nah," replied Jimmy. "They run the footage in slo-mo and everything, but you only see Reagan wince a bit. They say he got hit in the arm, but I can't see it. He just scrunches up his face and they push him in a limo."

My class was silent, disturbed, inward. I was rattled, feigning calm. I shuddered to think I would have to watch another Zapruder film. I remembered how my own seventh grade teacher had told us about Kennedy's assassination, how the only black girl in my class, Clemmy Carter, had wept openly and unashamedly. I remembered how awful I felt, registering the whole thing as some kind of sexual outrage.

I don't know why, perhaps it was my age, but the Kennedy assassination seemed pornographic to me, like a public castration, like some ugly obscenity had entered into history in a way even our parents could not deny—all those medical descriptions of entry and exit wounds, those horrific line drawings of his head and body that turned him into a kind of voodoo doll.

They wouldn't do that to Reagan. Surely we had learned. Surely this time, we knew what reels to run in a crisis. But what was I to say to the kids? What was my role as their teacher?

"I hope he's dead," announced Marlowe Lakes, always ready and willing to shock. "People die every day; no one cares unless you're rich or famous."

I couldn't tell at first if he was just seeking a reason not to care, or if he had himself suffered a death that had gone unnoticed.

"All violence is horrible," I said.

"Why are they always shot by deranged, lone assassins?" asked Bob Brown. "Do you think it was a conspiracy?"

"Yeah, by his P.R. man," suggested Marlowe. "They probably staged the whole thing just to make him more popular."

Marty Shuster rose to the president's defense. "They probably tried to kill him because he was helping the people too much. Defending the little guy."

I shuddered at the ignorance of this analysis.

"That guy could care less about the little guy!" replied Jim Bailey. "If the big boys wanted him dead, he'd BE dead. The videos would show a puff of red dust, and he'd be history. No, Reagan wasn't shot by any conspiracy; he was shot by some screw-off. Somebody like Marlowe."

Marlowe enjoyed the reference. "That's right," he announced. "I offed him, and I'd do it again."

"Shut up, Marlowe!" said Timmy Snider.

"Yeah, you loved that asshole!" replied Marlowe.

Timmy just repeated himself. "Shut up!"

They were seconds away from a fist fight.

"Now, now," I said. "That's enough!"

The class seemed torn between black humor, fear, and grief. What direction dare I take it? What lesson was unfolding here?

"From all the reports," I assured them, "Reagan is all right. The important thing to do right now is to watch what people say, remember what you are being told, register your reactions and those of other people, take the pulse of this national crisis, because there will be others."

"It just scares me," admitted Marty Shuster, "to think that everybody, even the president, is so vulnerable to violence."

"He should wear a bulletproof vest all the time," offered Timmy.

"Yeah, Timmy," Jim Bailey replied in disgust. "And maybe he could also wear a big plastic helmet with a face guard and a solid steel protective cup, and he could paint the cup red, white, and blue. And whenever he travels, he could go there in a giant bombproof Pyrex hamster bubble!"

I couldn't quite fathom where they were taking all this. What really concerned them?

"I feel like Piggy in *Lord of the Flies*," Jim admitted. "It's like everything is out of control and nobody listens to reason, and so the dumb guys push everybody around."

"Yeah, and what are you gonna do about it?" taunted Marlowe. "Cry?"

"No, I'm not gonna *cry*," replied Jim. "But I don't have to think it's cool. If it's all about guns and killing, and if guys like Marlowe are constantly screwing things up, why bother?"

Marlowe threw back his head.

"But it's not all guns and killing," I said. "Remember Simon in *Lord of the Flies*. He wanted everyone to go the mountaintop. If they had listened to him, they would have discovered the downed flyer and overcome their fears."

"But they didn't go to the mountaintop," insisted Marlowe. "And Simon ended up dead—just like Martin Luther King!"

We all thought about this for a second.

"Well, we all end up dead eventually," Jim Bailey finally countered. "At least Martin Luther King died for something, at least he was somebody."

"He was somebody all right," mocked Marlowe. "He was dead meat."

"Maybe so," I admitted. "But Martin Luther King was a man of character."

"A man of character?" Marlowe repeated. "What's *that*?"

It was a good question.

"It's someone who realizes that bullies are not to be admired, even if they cannot always be defeated," I said. "It is someone who has grown up, who stands up for others, who has become a human being."

"It's a person with a lot of money," quipped Marlowe.

"No," I said. "Money hasn't anything to do with it. There are a lot of rich cowards in the world."

"Like Marty!" shouted Marlowe.

"I'm not a coward! You are!"

Marty leaped across his desk and grabbed Marlowe's shoulder. They tumbled to the floor, knocking over a desk.

"Stop it!" I cried, as I pulled them apart. "*Stop* fighting."

"Why?" asked Marlowe—angry, defiant, holding back tears.

"Because it's stupid," I said. "Because it's just plain *stupid*!"

And I realized then that, on one level, that was really all the explanation I could give them. Nothing elaborate, just a firm and resolute affirmation of civilized life. Anything less was just plain *stupid*.

We turned to our literature lesson and read a few more chapters of *Lord of the Flies*.

The class didn't say much after the fight. They seemed emotionally spent.

After school, I noticed that Alphonse, the usually energetic neighborhood dog, was lying morosely at the end of the hall.

"What's wrong with Alphonse?" I asked the teacher who was cleaning erasers in the room next to mine.

"Oh, one of your students kicked him," he replied. "These kids can be *so* cruel."

I went home and watched the news clips of Reagan being shot. I must have seen it at least a dozen times in the space of two hours: forward, backward, in slow motion, with commentary and without. I was struck by the banality of the violence and the confusion. The images were without significant emotion—like tossed dummies.

I remembered, by contrast, the Zapruder film. How, as a child, I stared at the isolated frames in a 1964 yearbook, trying to locate the awful shot to the head—never realizing this frame had been removed by some well-meaning editor, although the written commentary mentioned it again and again.

The fact that the head shot was missing made it all that much more horrible to comprehend. The bright green grass behind the car, the blurred movements. Years later, when I saw the whole uncensored Zapruder film, I was shocked by the violence of the third shot and wondered how I might have taken it as an eleven-year-old boy traumatized enough by Kennedy's assassination. Would it have helped to have seen it? Probably not. I had seen enough. And like Jim Bailey, it would have made me suspicious of adults and of history. It would have made me wonder about growing up. It might have even driven me to kick the school dog.

Instead, I remember Jacqueline Kennedy. She was a mother figure to me then—a Madonna in a black veil—testifying to truths deeper than the fantastic, murderous history we were all living through. Her image saved me—perhaps, saved us all—kissing that casket in the great rotunda.

Brother Blake asked me if the students seemed "better" or "worse" than when I first started teaching.

"Better," I said.

"Wrong answer," he replied.

"Worse?" I tried.

"No," he said. "The more you grow as a teacher, the more you will realize that the humanity of your students is both better and worse than you can ever imagine. The human heart is vast."

11

Teaching Sex Education

We do not exist for ourselves alone, and it is only when we are fully convinced of this fact that we begin to love ourselves properly and thus also love others. What do I mean by loving ourselves properly? I mean, first of all, desiring to live, accepting life as a great good, not because of what it gives us, but because of what it enables us to give others.

Thomas Merton, *No Man Is an Island*

April

Marty Shuster's big brother, Marvin, was a frequent purchaser of pornographic magazines, and from time to time Marty would bring one to class. I'd confiscate it and send him to Strapp, who would return the magazine to Marty's parents and threaten to suspend him from school—but nothing ever happened.

"Ah, Mr. Inchausti," Marty would say, "don't tell me you don't like to look too."

The other kids were both fascinated and appalled by Marty's audacity and knowledge of forbidden realms. And I think it was this prestige that kept him bringing those magazines to school, even though he was risking expulsion.

Brother Blake suggested that I ask Marty if he was banging the magazine or if the magazine was banging him. "Tell him that he is being screwed, but he doesn't mind it because it feels so good!"

"It wouldn't bother him." I said. "He'd just say he was banging the magazine. He's proud of it. Pornography is adult literature to him. He likes to shock his more innocent peers."

But as outraged as I was, I had to admit that, as a graduate student, I did visit Little Joe Hombre's Topless Nightclub over on Stockton Boulevard, and, well, I guess I felt a bit hypocritical censoring Marty's sexual curiosity. So I asked Brother Blake his views on these matters.

"Concupiscence of the eyes," he said definitively. "Concupiscence of the eyes! The prurient gaze makes you look at things not for their truth or their reality, but to lose yourself in their evocative possibilities. The soul ceases to be centered within and searches each curve and crevice of shapely matter for a refuge from its chaos. What's wrong with this is that it is a futile search that only increases one's fascination with plummeting every mystery—the more one sees in this way the more one needs to see EVERY-THING in this way.

"The joke is that what one sees is not reality at all, but projected images of one's own lusts. Those magazines hurt boys because they addict them to illusion and teach them how *not* to see."

Blake pulled a slim volume off his bookshelf and thumbed through it. "Listen to what the Thomist Josef Pieper says about such illusory excitements:"

Behind their papery facade of ostentation lies nothingness. A "world" of at most one-day constructs that become insipid after just one-quarter of an hour and are thrown out like a newspaper that has been read or a magazine that has been paged through; a world before the revealing gaze of a sound spirit uninfected by contagion, shows itself to be like a metropolitan entertainment district in the harsh clarity of a winter morning: barren, bleak, and ghostly to the point of pushing one to despair.*

A Brief Reader on the Virtues of the Human Heart (San Francisco: Ignatius Press, 1991), p. 40.

"Isn't that wonderful writing?" Blake noted. "The destructive thing about pornography is that it addicts the students to distortions and dissimulation in sexual matters, making it difficult for them to see the personhood of women. And they need to be able to see *that* if they are ever going to understand their own sexuality."

"Well, that's wonderful theology," I demurred. "But the fact remains that that stuff is attractive to these kids, and discerning reality with a capital "R" is hardly their primary concern. These boys are not metaphysicians! Besides, aren't they attracted to pornography precisely because it *does* reveal a reality they are excluded from? Don't they seek it out because it helps them to uncover the mysteries of the opposite sex?"

"No," he said. "What they want to know are the real mysteries, not just the tease of a strip show. The real mysteries reside in the emotional depths, not in the shadow play of appearances. They all know this deep down, but the peekaboo of pornography confuses them.

"Look," he confessed. "I'm no saint. I too used my youth and sexuality as an intoxicant and so hit my late thirties like a brick wall. The problem is that, in our culture, we exploit our biologies, and so when we hit middle age, giving up our youth is as difficult as giving up 'smack.' We don't educate ourselves to move through physical pleasure to spiritual joy, to move through eros to charity. Pornography is just part of this miseducation. These young men need something stronger than titillation to sustain their joy in living past age thirty-five."

I was thinking about myself now, not Marty. How I had been educated to a lascivious eye. Had I been demeaned? Was I morally malformed?

"Does spiritual development actually possess compensations for the satiation of lust?" I asked.

"Beyond anything you can imagine," he said. "Here, you can borrow my copy of Aquinas."

Blake told me that the boys have a hard time realizing that a relationship is something you discover, not something you make happen.

"I tell them," he said, "to look up at the ceiling. What is its *relationship* to the wall? Or I ask them, 'What is the *relationship* between the floor and the feet of your desk?'

"Relationships are objective things, I tell them. They exist to be discovered. They cannot be forced. You cannot make the front wall connect with the rear wall—but you can see that they both connect at the ceiling.

"Forcing relationships between objects, or people, or even ideas, is a form of coercion. These boys have to be taught to stand back and let relationships reveal themselves, not force things to happen according to their will—that is sexual morality in a nutshell and the essence of common sense."

The students at St. Vincent's all take a special three-week course on health and sexuality. They have a rather clinical textbook which gives them all the facts anyone could ever need concerning birth control, sexually transmitted diseases, and the biology of reproduction. They even receive teachings as to the church's views on sexual morality. But, thanks to Brother Blake, their lessons also included stories and myths about relationships. One of his favorites was taken from a little anthology of myths. It was called, "What Do Women Want?"*

This is the famous tale of King Arthur and his trusty mate Sir Gawaine. One day during their travels, they come around a corner to discover a fire-breathing monster standing in their path. Unarmed, they must use their wits, and so King Arthur tells the monster that it would be unfair to simply eat them on the spot. The monster should pose some riddle to them. If they solve it, he must let them go free. If they fail, he can eat them both without protest.

The monster agrees and asks them, "What do women want?"

King Arthur and Sir Gawaine confer, decide this is too difficult a question, and ask for more time.

_____

*Barbara Stanford, *Myths and Modern Man* (New York: Washington Square Press, 1972).

"I will give you one year," the monster replies. "Exactly one year from today, you must meet me at this very spot and give me your answer. If you are right, you will live. If not, I will eat you." And so the men are set free.

Sir Gawaine is confident.

"This will be easy," he says. "We will just take a survey of all the women we see, and by the end of the year, we will know what women want."

So they immediately begin, asking an old woman on the road what she wants. "I want to be left alone," she tells them.

They ask a young girl. "I want a handsome lover," she replies.

They ask a farmer's wife. "I want a lot of money," she says.

"This is not working," King Arthur observes. "Every woman we ask is unique. Each one has a different desire. We will never find out!"

And so a year passes, and the two must return to meet the monster, no wiser as to what women want than the day they set out on their quest. Suddenly, a witch appears before them and tells them that she knows the answer to the riddle.

"Tell us," they plead.

"I will tell you only if Sir Gawaine agrees that, after the monster releases him, he will marry me."

"I can't let you do that," King Arthur tells Gawaine. "This woman is a hideous hag."

"It's our only hope," Gawaine replies. Then, turning to the hag, Gawaine promises, "I will marry you. Now, what do women want?"

"They want power over men," the witch replies.

"Is that it?" The two men are amazed by the simplicity of the answer, but they tell it to the monster, and he lets them go. Now, however, Gawaine must marry the witch, and she demands a huge public ceremony. All of Gawaine's enemies and so-called friends attend the wedding to mock and humiliate him.

But then, a strange thing happens. After the ceremony, the witch asks Sir Gawaine to kiss her. "Do I have to?" he asks.

"It's customary," she says.

And so, to hoots and catcalls, Gawaine kisses the hag full on the lips, and she is instantly transformed into a beautiful princess.

"What is this?" Sir Gawaine asks.

"Well," the hag explains, "when I was young, I was transformed into a witch by a powerful wizard, and he said the only way I could ever be changed back was if I married and kissed one of the Knights of the Round Table, and now that has happened. The only catch is that I can be a beautiful woman for only twelve hours of the day; the other twelve, I will remain a hag. Which would you prefer? That I be beautiful during the day, so that your friends and enemies can see me and envy you, or that I be beautiful at night, when we are alone together in our bedroom?"

"You have been a hag for so long, and this has been such an unjust fate, why don't *you* decide?" Sir Gawaine replies.

And then, a thunderbolt crashes overhead, and a shiver passes through the beautiful princess.

"Now I can be beautiful twenty-four hours a day, because the second part of the curse could only be lifted if I married a Knight of the Round Table and I got my way with him."

And so the story ends, with an affirmation of mutual self-sacrifice and common accord, dramatizing the necessity of giving up power in order that it might be given back to you.

"These are the lessons in sexual maturity these kids need," Blake declared, "along with an awareness of the superiority of latex condoms."

12

Teaching Literature: Making the World Safe for Franz Kafka

Sir Thomas More: Why not be a teacher? You'd be a fine teacher. Perhaps even a great one.
Richard Rich: And if I was, who would know it?
Sir Thomas More: You, your pupils, God. Not a bad public, that.
                                    Richard Bolt, *A Man for All Seasons*

April

One of the unique premises of the humanities program at St. Vincent's was its idea of basic skills. Writing, reading, and arithmetic did not qualify because they were secondary elaborations upon a more basic activity: perception. In other words, in place of a teaching method, the humanities at St. Vincent's operated on a poetic. It sought not so much to inform as to evoke, and this led to a very different way of teaching both literature and the Bible.

The ninth grade literature program, for example, began with certain definitions that were, in fact, moral-aesthetic distinctions of relative complexity. The students were told that they were not to *behave*, *listen*, or *write* in class. Instead, they were to *act*, *hear*, and *compose*. Talking was for recess—an emotional give-and-take—but in class, one *spoke*. That is to say, one made public statements and claims about reality. *Writing*, likewise, was for notes to your friends, but *composing* was a craft. *Listening* was a passive act; *hearing*, a form of cocreation. And if one *behaved*, one was merely doing the expected. To *act* was to be responsible for one's deeds.

Students were also warned not to *think*. *Thinking* was like worrying—turning things over and over in one's mind. Instead they were to *reason*, that is, systematically consider the truth of specific claims.

When explaining the nature of figurative language, I would begin by telling my students a story from the "Star Trek" television show. Captain Kirk and Lieutenant Spock find themselves face-to-face with one of the "portals of the universe." They can get no tricorder readings of the thing; it defies analysis.

"Tell us what you are!" commands Spock.

The portal shimmers and glows, and then a voice finally emerges from it.

"I am, and I am not. I have been, and I shall always be. I am the wall, and I am the door."

Captain Kirk is not impressed by this answer.

"Don't give us any of your double-talk. We are *men*. Tell us *who* you are!"

The portal shimmers some more and then replies, "I am the Alpha and the Omega. I am the end and the beginning. I am the portal of the universe."

By this time, Kirk is mad.

"I told you to tell us what you *are*. We have no time for your poetry. Tell us now in simple and direct language, or we will *have* to use force."

With this, Kirk takes out his fazer and points it at the portal.

The portal shimmers again and then replies, "I am telling you who I am in the most literal language your puny human brains can comprehend!"

At this, Kirk and Spock leap through the portal and end up in some frozen wasteland. It takes them the rest of the show to get back to their ship. But the lesson about metaphor had been made. A metaphor is not language disguised or dressed up, but language denuded and made plain in an attempt to clarify a difficult reality.

It is an attempt to communicate new ideas in the most direct language our "puny human brains" can comprehend.

Kirk, who represents the will, and Spock, who represents reason, simply cannot understand the meaning of the poetic image, and so they end up lost and disoriented.

I would tell the students that when I was a boy I used to open my best friend's locker and read the love letters he would send to his girlfriend. To signify his love, he would mark the bottom of the page with XXXXXXXs and OOOOOOOOs. Soon, Xs and Os filled the paper. After about three letters like this, he decided that there must be an easier way to express the magnitude of his love, and so he ventured a metaphor.

"If they took my love," he wrote, "and loaded it onto boxcars, those boxcars would be so numerous that they would circle the globe three times."

Now, this was awful love poetry, because the images connote all the wrong associations. Love loaded into boxcars is rough, dirty, noisy, unkempt, and gross. Which is, come to think of it, probably not unlike my friend's own lustful teenage longings! And the idea of circling the globe three times calls to mind those old black-and-white documentary films on bauxite production in Argentina: "If all the tungsten in Mozambique was placed end to end . . ." And so my friend's love, as he described it, was ugly and statistical, unkempt, and passionless—exactly the wrong set of traits to win the heart of a romantic young girl.

To do better, he would need to go somewhere else for his images, nature perhaps. "My love is as vast as the distance between two stars." T. S. Eliot called this search for the correct image the search for the "objective correlative."

The first "long" book we read together was William Golding's powerful parable *Lord of the Flies*. It's a novel about a group of British prep school boys who find themselves abandoned on an island after a plane crash and must fend for themselves without adults.

At first, they experience the absence of constraints as a liberation and live a kind of utopian existence of leisure and play. But as the survival demands of the environment become more pressing, the boys break up into two gangs: one primitive, savage, and fascist; the other clinging to civilized traditions in an attempt to emulate their parents' democratic institutions.

A virtual war breaks out between these two groups, with various characters taking on the roles of various human and psychological archetypes. Jack, the lean, trim, warrior, is the advocate of primitive violence, passion, and impulse. The fat, bespectacled Piggy is the intellectual—advocate of adult standards, memory, and tradition. Ralph is Jack's rational counterpart—a leader keyed to realities, common sense, compromise, and collective action. And then there is Simon: visionary, outcast, scapegoat, and martyr—advocate of exploration and the educated imagination. Simon wants to take all the kids to the top of the mountain so that they can all see for themselves that the downed flyer lying dead is no bogey man, and by so doing calm the growing hysteria, panic, and paranoia of the lost boys. But Simon is ignored, finally killed, and the boys degenerate into barbarians.

When the adults arrive, the boys cry over what they have become, over the evils they have discovered in themselves. But Golding makes it clear that the adult world is really no better; it too has been torn apart by war, and the adults who rescue the boys are soldiers and survivors of a nuclear conflict. The boys will be going home to a different world in more ways than one.

Now, to read this book in the setting of a ninth grade classroom—which itself is perpetually on the verge of anarchy—is to read it not only as a parable of the modern but also as a mimetic description of teenage life. We had plenty of Jacks in our school—bullies who lived by the code of intimidation. We had our share of Piggys too—overprotected kids who were moral weaklings; intelligent but cowardly. We had our Ralphs—honest, brave, searching souls, confused by the chaos around them but willing to try to make some sense of it, willing at least to try to build a bridge toward civilization. And we had one or two Simons—dreamy, inward, imaginative, almost invisible kids, who moved through the hallways as if in conversation with some other reality, capable it seemed of walking through walls and disappearing before our very eyes. And then there were the rest, who collected around these teenage archetypes like variations on a theme: friends, best friends, archenemies, and mascots.

But if *Lord of the Flies* held a mirror up to their teenage world, our next book, *Siddhartha*, revealed an alternative to it and provided a picture of life as a heroic quest for truth and meaning. The prose was so spare, and the chapters so short, that we read the book quickly but discussed it for hours.

For boys, becoming a hero is about as full a life as they can imagine, but *Siddhartha* teaches that heroism is an adolescent aspiration. The real achievements in life come *after the heroics*, and they are expressed in service and humility. It was the ferryman in *Siddhartha* who lived the exemplary life. And, in a way, teachers are ferrymen—traveling back and forth from the shore of one generation to the shore of the next, not really going anywhere, perpetually in transit but always present.

My only problem teaching *Siddhartha* was that Bob Brown kept reading *Mad Magazines* in class instead of the text, so I confronted him one day.

"You know," I said. "Don Martin [that nutty *Mad Magazine* writer who created the comic strip "Spy vs. Spy"] has probably read *Siddhartha*."

"No way," Bob said.

"No? Don Martin's a creative and clever guy. I'm sure he reads books. I'm *sure* he's read *Siddhartha*. In fact, he probably read it when he was just about your age."

"No, no, no," Bob insisted, shaking his head.

"Okay, if you're so sure," I said, "then why don't you write him a letter and ask him? Tell him your English teacher wants to know if he has ever read *Siddhartha*."

Bob wrote the letter.

We waited for several months, and there was no reply until the week before the last day of school, Bob came running up to me with a letter on official *Mad Magazine* stationery. It read:

Dear Bob:

Thank you for your interest in Don Martin. But we have to inform you that not only has Don Martin never read *Siddhartha*, Don Martin cannot read!

Well, so much for my attempt to bring popular culture into the curriculum. I should have known better than to think my authority as a teacher would be enough to shake the editors out of their satiric mentality.

And yet, the letter had a wonderful effect upon Bob. He was really impressed that the editors of *Mad Magazine* would be so consistently ironic. It sealed his confidence in them. Don Martin had absolutely refused to take himself seriously. And so he remained wonderful. Funny. Life-giving. And in a strange way, his reply had also elevated *Siddhartha* in Bob's mind as something outside the comic keen of his favorite magazine.

Next we read *The Martian Chronicles* by Ray Bradbury as part of our social studies unit on American history and the westward expansion. I told the boys that Ray Bradbury was doing more than just telling us fantastic stories about creatures who never existed; he was also trying to tell us, in the most literal language our "puny human brains" could comprehend, the meaning of conquest.

Just as a novel about St. Vincent's may be a warning to your friends not to come here, so Bradbury's book may be a warning as to how *not* to colonize space, how *not* to move into the future.

The progression of our reading assignments was ingenious. We had begun with "the image"—pictures, cartoons, lines from poems; moved on to symbols—the crucifix, Madonna and Child, the American flag; progressed to the fable via Aesop and to the parable via Matthew. *Lord of the Flies* advanced us to full-blown narrative and served as a bridge between the fable and the myth of *Siddhartha*. And now, with *The Martian Chronicles*, we had arrived at the novel as a criticism of myths: the myths of manifest destiny, scientific progress, capitalism, and Western cultural superiority.

The Martian Chronicles contains twenty-six stories organized around the topics of invasion and exploration, colonization, and apocalypse. Mars is the New World, the new frontier, lush virgin territory, and yet like *our* frontier already occupied, already ancient, with a culture going back a million years. The Martians are the Mayans, the Indians, subdued by the white man. And as wave after wave of settlers arrives, each wave has its own story, its own crimes, its own discoveries.

The Martian Chronicles tells the story of our future as a repetition of our past and so serves as a warning of how not to proceed. It is Ray Bradbury's sermon to technological America, a reminder that in between our fantasies of a utopian past and our dreams of a utopian future lies a very problematic present. Our tragedy as a people may come from our inability to imagine the greatness of other cultures and other worlds.

It is a book about the need for reverence, and the difficulty we have as a nation acquiring it. If our desires reach out for things that have no meaning for the growth of our spirit, if we lose ourselves in ambitions and illusions, in the end, our lives will become forces for destruction. However talented we may be or advanced in our technology, we will find ourselves aliens from ourselves and from God.

As we read the book, we began to formulate a new repertoire of class mottos and figures of speech. I would sometimes say, "I feel like I am from Mars!" And they would immediately understand that I felt like a creature from another world—an older world with more ancient sympathies.

This incorporation of textual images into our everyday speech allowed the students to see the way literature works as an ongoing commentary on life—as a system of images, as a language in itself.

If Marty "spaced out" during a class discussion, I could now signal him back to earth by saying, "Well, Marty, are you on the expedition?" The phrase would reverberate with symbolic significance.

"Yeah, Colonel," he would reply. "You want to go hunting Martians?"

The novel, in other words, became our class theme, the code through which we deciphered events, the medium through which we understood *everything*. We didn't simply read *The Martian Chronicles*—we spoke it; we thought it; we lived it. Just as we had done with *Lord of the Flies* and *Siddhartha*. Only now, we had entered into a more conscious criticism of social mythology.

Prior to reading *The Martian Chronicles* with my class, I had considered Ray Bradbury a second-rate writer, sentimental, nostalgic, the Norman Rockwell of science fiction. And I had never liked science fiction much anyway for its gimmicky, facile theorizing and its use of all those weird proper names: "Gimlack Three," "Queen Zina of Tarse," "The Moons of Platitudia."

But now, I saw things differently. *The Martian Chronicles* was not a great book, but the genre of the novel was itself a great idiom. For those who had eyes to see, there were treasures to be found here. Besides, we had poured so much of ourselves into that book that it took on a second life as a cultural document in a living community and thereby became a reservoir of images that far transcended the specific intentions of the author.

After *The Martian Chronicles*, we read *Night* by Elie Wiesel. And as most literature teachers will confess, sometimes when we are trying to explain a work, we are visited by a peculiar eloquence not entirely our own, and the book we are teaching not only teaches itself but lifts us up to its own heights. I remember the scene at the end of the fourth section with its chilling description of the hanging of three prisoners—one a young boy who did not immediately die because his body was too light to snap his neck. The other prisoners are forced to march by the corpses and this child's half-dead body. Someone asks, "Where is God now?" And Wiesel hears a voice within answer, "Where is He? Here He is—He is hanging here on the gallows."*

The students were puzzled by this line and wanted to know what it meant. I was a little self-conscious about presuming to "teach" this book, especially to such callow youth. But I took courage from an account I had read of Wiesel's own appearance before a high school in New York, where he answered each and every question posed to him with patience and complete honesty. One of the kids had asked him to describe the looks on the faces of the guards as they committed their atrocities. Wiesel answered that he didn't look into their eyes; they were his masters. I could at least try to be as honest about my own experience. Besides, there is something about Wiesel's prose—its honesty, its refusal to "protect" the reader from the realities of life, however harsh—that immediately earned the trust of these adolescent boys. They felt elevated by his respect for them as readers. Of all of the books we read that year, *Night* was the one they took most seriously. They wanted to talk about it; they needed to talk about it. But they didn't know what to say.

"What does that mean that God is hanging on the gallows?" they asked.

I could have offered some glib remark about the death of God, but I decided to be honest. "I don't know."

"Did it really happen?"

"Yes."

"This is really a weird book!" And I could see by their expressions that they meant awesome, uncanny, disturbing.

Finally, one student ventured his own version of a "Catholic" interpretation. "I think he was talking about Jesus. The three men, the suffering one in the middle—its like Jesus on the cross."

"This is a child," I said. "A million of them were killed by the Nazis. It's not Jesus."

"But it's a Jewish boy. Isn't it a symbol?"

---

*Elie Wiesel, *Night*, trans. Marion Wiesel (New York: Summit Books, 1988), p. 209.

I was uneasy saying "no." All literature is, in some sense, symbolic, since it synthesizes the abstract and the concrete into typical representations, but *Night* was different. It was testimony and witness—an attempt not to betray those who died—and I wanted to live up as best I could to Wiesel's intentions. "No," I said finally. "It is not a symbol. At least not the kind of symbol we are used to talking about. It would be just as accurate to say Jesus is a symbol for this child than that this child is a symbol for Jesus." I could tell by their quizzical faces that they weren't getting me. I was sounding heretical. Perhaps even a bit crazy.

"Look," I continued, "its really a question of what is most real. In this story, nothing is more real than the death of this child. I think for Wiesel, Jesus' death is not any more or less important than the death of two million Jewish children. And we are meant to experience the horror of the camps through his precise particularizations. To see this child as a *symbol* would be to forget his humanity, his precious irreplaceability, his never-again, individual character."

"But then what's it *mean*?" they asked again. "What is it supposed to mean *to us*?"

"The fact that a death like this could happen—did happen—confronts us with certain uncomfortable truths about life and what it means to be a human being, such as the vulnerability of the innocent before those who would be gods. But there isn't always a universal truth in every situation. Perhaps the point here is more particular and temporal: that death in the camps was never symbolic, that it was always personal, insufferable, beyond mythic explanation."

The class didn't say anything. I wondered if they followed me. I wondered if I followed myself. But I could tell they were thinking.

"So you mean that this death doesn't mean anything *good*?" asked Albert Perez, straining to make sense of it all. "That it's not part of some point he's trying to make, that its a total waste and *that's* what it means?"

"Sort of," I replied. "I don't think it was a total waste, because it did affect people, change lives, forced us to examine our consciences, but these effects are never to be seen as worth any fraction of the price that was paid for them. This death is not redemptive in any Christian sense. It is one of the worst things that human beings have ever done."

"Even worse than satanic tortures and sexual mutilations?" asked Marty Shuster. I could tell by this question that the conversation had become quite real for him.

"There were tortures and mutilations in the camps. Besides, this was government-sponsored torture and mutilation aimed at an entire ethnic population, endorsed by 'good' citizens as prudent political policy. In this sense, it was the worst thing civilized man ever did."

"So what can *we* do about it? Its over. Most of these people are dead."

"They live in memory and conscience. Their ghosts haunt our lives. They are as real as we are, maybe even more real," I said.

"How can they be more real than we are?" Jim asked.

"They died for who they were. They died because they were Jews. We would do well to stand for so much."

"So the whole book is symbolic; the boy's death is a symbol," Jim insisted.

I attempted one last time to explain the distinction. "No, its a memory. And now, in a way, it's our memory too, so we've got to live with it, and we have to live lives of substance to be worthy of it. If we live, we have obligations as survivors not to betray the humanity of those who came before us by belittling our own."

"But how do you do that? How do you live a life of substance?"

"For a start," I said, "you can read the rest of this book." They laughed and took this as the typical manipulative evasion of an English teacher, but I meant it.

Often, in teaching some sublime text, we find ourselves carried away by its beauty and goodness, and by the grace of God, the words of angels appear in our mouths, and we inspire others to fine and wonderful aspirations. But later, after school, we come down. How dare we speak so movingly? How dare we presume such offices? And so, in a peculiar psychological paradox, we feel shame over our finest lectures.

This happened to me once after I had given a particularly passionate interpretation of the beatitudes. I thought back upon what I had said—thinking that I might be feeling guilt for having misrepresented the material. But as far as I could tell, I had been fair and honest—and even more than that, I had been eloquent. Why, then, the shame? What was embarrassing me? Why could I remember my presentation with only fear and loathing?

Brother Blake explained it to me this way: "Take someone famous, like John F. Kennedy, Jr. He was born into immense energies—mythic powers—that must have startled him. The most beautiful girls fall at his feet. People far brighter than he stutter in his presence. He could be tempted to think that all that juice comes from *him*. But it doesn't really. It's a kind of energy he finds himself living inside as a result of his history, his personality, his good looks—in short, his fate.

"Those of us outside such power zones accidently enter them from time to time. We star in a play or give a great lecture, and suddenly people relate to us differently, as if we were larger. We have our fifteen minutes of fame. And our first reaction is to shy away from the attention because we know all too well that this power doesn't come from us—that we are merely caught in the winds of larger forces. But to dismiss these powers *because* they don't come from us is as much an act of egotism as thinking that they *do* come from us. The point isn't that we should use only those virtues that we *possess*; the point is that we should wake up to the virtues and powers all around us, so that they can be responsibly employed. This is not magic; it is existentialism. And it is an expression of profound humility."

And so the cure for this failure of confidence, insofar as there is one, is to realize that it is good to do good, even if we cannot embody it. That for teachers to dramatize the ideals they teach—to impersonate the wise, if only for the space of a single lesson—is not an act of hubris or usurpation, but a natural and noble, honorable deed. Part of one's job. And if the sublime is to remain alive in education, we must dare to inspire, even if we ourselves are social outcasts with little money and less prestige.

So now, when I feel those pangs of shame, I register them differently. They are warnings—not that I am posturing, but that I don't trust myself enough.

13

Higher Education

It is not by reading or historical study that we become wise in the science of God; such methods alone produce but a vain, confused, and self-inflating science. What instructs us is what happens to us from moment to moment; that is what forms in us that experiential knowledge which Jesus Christ willed to acquire before he taught it. This was indeed the only knowledge in which, according to the expression in the Gospel, he could grow, because being God there was no degree of speculative science he did not possess. But if this knowledge was useful to the Incarnate Word himself, for us it is absolutely necessary if we wish to speak to the heart of the persons whom God sends us.

Father J. P de Caussade, S. J., *Self-Abandonment to Divine Providence*

May

The freshman humanities program had a faculty development budget of exactly $350, so we decided to spend the money on a one-day trip to the Jung Institute in San Francisco to hear lectures by Joseph Campbell and James Hillman on "The Image of the Bull in World Mythology."

For Campbell, the bull was an image of material reality—and the bullfighter and bull jumper emblematic of our human capacity to transcend the finite. The bull jumpers of Crete had to learn to *grab the bull by the horns* and, in a deft maneuver requiring both risk and dexterity, flip themselves over the bull's head. In a similar act, the matador must *pass through the horns of a dilemma* to pierce the bull between the eyes. All these images warn of the dangers of positioning yourself too much to the left or the right, of not taking things head on, of refusing to seize the day resolutely.

We took these admonitions as direct advice as to how to teach the ninth grade. The bull we faced was the stubborn adolescent will. And, like matadors, we sought out tips for skillfully avoiding its horns. Throughout the lecture, whenever Campbell made a particularly applicable point, such as his depiction of the bull as powerful but uncoordinated, fast but maladapted, Mike Morton, our history teacher, would smile at me as if to say, "See? He knows all about our students, and yet he's never met them."

Mike was a Campbell devotee, and although I admired *Hero with a Thousand Faces* and took wisdom wherever I could find it, I was always a bit less enthusiastic. Campbell wouldn't have lasted very long in our classrooms, I suspected. His views were refined, his aesthetic spiritualized. Our students—our little bulls—could not be so easily transcended. Besides, to my mind, Campbell tended to misread the Hebrew scriptures, interpreting them always in the light of the New Testament and so discounting their radical existential thrust and *this* worldly concern for justice. He saw them as essentially defenses of "the law" and advanced his more flexible Hindu-Christian mono-myth in their place.

So even though I marveled at the connections he made between myth and experience, I also suspected that they might be a bit too easy and that my life was more like a novel than a mythology, its plot more Hebraic than Pauline.

Hillman's talk was more to my taste—witty and heterodox. He asked what has become of the bull, which is the same thing as asking what has become of reality as a full, material, inescapable blunt force. He argued that the modern world has ground it into hamburger. Processed it out of existence. Tamed it beyond measure. And now suffers from its absence. The memory of its divinity remains in our unconscious fast-food dreams—Burger King, Dairy Queen, the King Combo, and the Burger Supreme.

He claimed that technology has cut us off from experience. Geometry once linked numbers to shapes. Algebra was a move into abstraction. Calculus abstracted the abstractions. Until now we think in the abbreviated language of technological mnemonics, ICBMs and EIRs. The psychological effect of this move into abstraction has been profound, leading us to seek the displaced concrete in a variety of substitute realities—television, fantasy, magic, and psychosis. What's left of reality now resides in what people call "bullshit," dreams, small talk, side issues, private perceptions—*literature*.

On the drive back home, Mike continued to express his enthusiasm for Campbell's analysis, and I continued to resist.

"It's all there," he said. "They told the story of what we do!"

"Well, sort of," I protested arrogantly. "It's part of what we do. I think in some ways, we are beyond them."

I loved Mike because he not only tolerated such crazy talk, he also enjoyed it, thrived on it, dove into the speculation—demanding that I explain myself.

"We *do* what they talk about," I explained. "*We* are the agents of the spirit. We meet the bull everyday. We are the matadors of the classroom, and so what Campbell says always strikes me as the most meager approximation of what art, ideas, and culture *are*. He's 'right' only because he is so general and so sweeping. He doesn't compose the mythology of his experience; he lets out the seams of myth to include the stories of our times."

Mike was thoughtful for a moment. "The ancient myths *are* the stories of our times," he said.

"Maybe," I replied, "maybe not. The problem with Campbell is that he just assumes this connection, when the whole point of living the spiritual life is to forge it."

"But he *says* that!" protested Mike. "That's what his book *Creative Mythology* is all about. How modernity is the quest for mythology, and how that quest makes up our contemporary identities. There is a story from the Balinese . . ."

It was a wonderful moment the way Mike fell back upon myth to defend the fullness of Campbell's witness, and yet I suspected the flexibility of Campbell's approach all the more. These were not ideas that bore down on the present, that compelled ethical choices. They were assaults upon blind literalism, encouragements to transcend. But what I needed, and I guess what I was asking Mike for at the time but didn't realize, was something else, maybe even something *less*. What I needed were ways to embrace the suffering and confusion before me. I needed lessons in finding happiness in particular sorrows, in the boredom and the terror on a specific fourteen-year-old boy's face.

Campbell, to me, had it only half right. Yes, my students were archetypal, but that told me nothing about their radically existential, one-of-a-kind promise and pain. I could encounter *that* only one-on-one inside the classroom. And, as helpful as the monomyth was in describing the psychology of that place, as a teacher-warrior, I was still alone.

Predicting and describing are different from doing and creating, and when I walked into that classroom, I stepped over the threshold from theory into practice, from mythology into life, from philosophical clarity into experiential confusion. My ability to embrace the mysterious reality of experience (its existential "weight") made me feel as if I had been graced with a form of second sight, where every idea revealed itself as a tactic and every fact a trace of some larger thought.

As a practicing classroom teacher, I cut through bullshit with a butter knife, and when I walked down the halls at school, it was as if invisible rays shot out at me from all directions, bringing revelation upon revelation.

If I opened a book, it was as if I could see through it. Everything was grist for my teacherly mill! I had become a teacher living within a creative passion and not feeding off anyone else's. I had found the grace in my difficult vocation, and I was surprised to discover Brother Blake had noticed it and jokingly remarked that he saw I had become "enlightened."

But I didn't feel enlightened; I felt merely as if I had finally begun to perceive. Before, I merely *thought*; now I knew things. Before, I spoke mostly to create impressions; now I spoke mostly to dispel them. I was no longer a seeker, I was a finder, just like Lao Tzu! Or so it seemed.

The next week, I was going to lunch after a particularly success-ful class period when Brother Blake caught the confidence in my step.

"You must really be a great teacher," he said. "I can tell by the way you are walking that you are really hot stuff."

"Ah, get off my case, Brother," I pleaded. "Can't I enjoy even one victory?"

"Well," he said. "If you take credit for the good days, you are going to have to take credit for the bad days too. Our task is to serve. One day, we serve them spaghetti; the next day, we serve them filet mignon; the next day, macaroni and cheese. But *they* choose what they are going to eat. Don't identify with the results!"

One day, one of the professors at the university was called out of town to give a public lecture, and knowing I had done some work in intellectual history in graduate school, she asked me to substitute for her two night classes: "The Modern Temper" and "Introduction to Literature." Her topic for the "Modern Temper" class for this week was Freud.

I accepted her offer with a mixture of excitement and resent-ment. Here she was making, what seemed to me, lots of money as a tenured, full-time professor, and I was going to be lucky to get so much as a complimentary bottle of wine for my troubles. I felt honored and exploited at the same time. Still, it would give me a chance to try out some of the skills I had learned at St. Vincent's in a university setting.

I began thinking about what I was going to say. Freud is a vast subject, and so I sat down and jotted out a few of Freud's greatest

ideas. I thought about showing the class how they defended
themselves against substitute teachers and guest lecturers—how
they would probably cling to libidinal ties established with their
absent professor, no matter how inept or mean she actually was.
Except for those who had yet to work through their Oedipal
conflicts. They would side with the substitute, seeking in me—the
new teacher—evidence that their absent teacher was wicked or
stupid. In either case, Freud's basic idea that we relive our experiences with our parents in our projections upon others would
be confirmed.

When I walked into the class, there was a chaos of over forty
people—all of them buzzing around, asking questions about tests,
finals, returned papers, quizzes, the whole trash can of college
concerns. I noted that, in high school, the students tell you straight-
out if they find you boring or irrelevant; in college, they lie. They
feign interest; they tax your credulity.

I felt smug and superior and terrified. I had hoped to be the
surprise of their lives—the first professor to make Freud come
alive for them, to make his ideas important, to turn some of them,
maybe just one of them, into a philosopher. But most of these
students just wanted to know what was going to be on the test so
they could go home.

I asked them for a synopsis of the class so far: "What is the
modern temper?" One of the students recited a list of themes—
everything from the death of God to the discovery of the unconscious. They seemed to be just words, and I didn't know how to
respond to these glib half-truths. It was all too pat and comfortable to be the *real* modern temper. It was a state college version
of the modern temper—a parody of deep thought, boredom
before the abyss, charlatanism, a simulcrum of understanding.

An older returning student, who should have known better,
cheerfully told me that "in today's postmodern world, not only
is God dead, but people are so advanced that they play God
themselves—they decide life and death issues without flinching,
they are beyond good and evil."

I didn't really disagree with him; it was just that he announced this triumph of nihilism so matter of factly as if it were a truism and heralded a coming age of liberation. I was horrified and suggested that awe before the universe and before God was a wonderful thing, and that if the "Modern Temper" trashed it, then maybe it was a dubious achievement.

"Have you read Chris Grisom's *You Are God?*" he asked. "It will explain everything."

I shuddered. New Age Nietzsches worried about quiz scores. Teaching-credential candidates bored by nihilism. The "Modern Temper" reduced to a few slogans and cliches. I wasn't up to this; I was better off teaching ninth grade.

For the "Introduction to Literature" class, I decided to use a different approach. Instead of the Socratic dialogue, I would do what I did at St. Vincent's—tell stories. The critic Harold Bloom said that the best response to a poem is another poem, so maybe the best response to a work of fiction is a story of one's own.

Today's text was Chekhov's short story "Gooseberries." If you don't know the story, it is about a veterinarian, Ivan Ivanovich, who visits a country estate with his friend Burkin, a high school teacher. In the course of their visit, Ivan tells his hosts and his friend the story of his brother, Nikolai, who was a petty bureaucrat in a government post with a dream of owning his own country estate with a duck pond, kitchen garden, and gooseberry bushes. After a long life of parsimony and narrow self-interest, he finally attains his goal and invites Ivan to have dinner with him.

For dessert, they have gooseberries. Ivan finds them sour, but his brother eats them with relish. Ivan is repulsed by his brother's unthinking greed and willingness to ignore the truth of things. The dinner is a revelation for Ivan, because he realizes he too has led a petty, self-interested life.

After telling this story, Ivan turns to his friend Burkin and to his host and pleads, "Don't be calm and contented, don't let yourself be put to sleep! While you are young, strong, and confident, be not weary of well doing! There is no happiness, and there ought not to be; but if there is a meaning and an object in life, that meaning and object is not our happiness, but something greater and more rational. Do good!"

But his friend and his host don't even discuss the accuracy of his observations and instead turn their attentions to the pretty servant girl and to accounts of elegant men and fashionable women. Ivan eventually goes to bed, in the richly appointed room, and as he pulls up his quilt from inside the warm, clean linen, he sighs, "Lord, forgive us sinners!"

"Well, what are we to make of this?" I asked the class. "Ivan Ivanovich has told us earlier in the story that nothing is so obscene as a contented, happy man, and that there ought to be someone with a hammer standing behind every contented man, banging it against the wall just to remind him that there is suffering in the world. But there is no man with the hammer, he laments, and so the happy man continues on in his ignorance until he gets sick and dies and no one notices. Such is Chekhov's vision of the spiritual blindness of the world."

To get this across, I described to them the General Mills television commercial for specialty coffees: a woman is sitting on her back porch in mild reflection, her husband appears out of nowhere and asks her how she is feeling. And she replies, "Oh, I don't know—it's just us, the kids, this house, my new job—it's all so wonderful; I just want it to last."

The husband says, "I'll go get some coffee."

And the voices of a choir come out of the stratosphere, singing, "Cel-a-brate the mo-ments of your life!"

"Now," I asked, "if Chekhov had written that commercial, if Ivan Ivanovich had been that woman's husband, what would he have said? I'll tell you what he would have said: he would have told her point-blank that it's not going to last, that she and he and the kids were all going to die someday, that the house will be rubble, that her job will go to someone not yet out of grammar school, that all around them lies the abyss, momentous human suffering, pain and injustice—and no goddamn cup of coffee is going to make it go away! To celebrate such moments of contentment is obscene. The only answer is not to live for yourself, but for a purpose. The only rational response to the pain of moral conscience is to do good. Nothing else makes sense, nothing else really matters."

They laughed, so I knew I had brought home the point.

"But what about the ending of 'Gooseberries'?" they asked. "Why does Ivan just go to bed, and why does he love the linens?"

I told them about a colleague at St. Vincent's, Dave Rockman, a Vietnam veteran, who, upon first returning from overseas, was outraged to find people playing tennis. "There is a war going on," he thought to himself. "How can you people be so insensitive as to play tennis? For God's sake, for your own sacred honor, STOP PLAYING TENNIS!!!!!!!" This is Ivan Ivanovich's consciousness—the consciousness which is a disease.

Dave also told me of going to the supermarket and seeing the riches there: rows and rows of food, a hundred different kinds of bread, a hundred different kinds of coffee, and people dropping all this stuff in little carts as if they had a right to it, as if it was the most natural thing in the world. And then these shoppers would have the audacity to argue with one another over whether to get chocolate cake or donuts. He remembers feeling his flesh crawl with revulsion as he wondered how these people could believe they were alive. Didn't they know other people were dying for what they believed, suffering to make the world a better place? Didn't they care? Did they think they deserved to profit from such sacrifices, or that they were worthy of them?

Such a perception was similar to Ivan Ivanovich's epiphany at his brother's dinner table, and then when he realizes that he is no better, that he too is living for himself and his own sensual life, he is struck by such shame and self-loathing that he cries out to God for forgiveness, just as he cried out to his companions not to be content with life.

But this consciousness passes; it fades. Dave adapted. In time, he got used to supermarkets, and he learned to find tennis normal.

But in adapting, in finding happiness again, had he lost consciousness?

I asked these questions and told these stories, and the students opened up with stories of their own. About how repelled one of them felt upon seeing Hugh Hefner's wedding photos—looking into the aged, collapsing face of a man who had lived for pleasure and seeing an empty shell, a grotesque, with his fading bunny beside him, unairbrushed, makeup ridden, smiling from ear to ear with a mansion behind her. Another student spoke of how embarrassed he was when his dad sat down to Thanksgiving dinner one year and gleefully announced, "I wonder what the poor people are doing tonight?"

And there were defenses of the sensual life and of Nikolai: "at least he did something," "at least he acted," "at least he *thought* he was happy," "he tried being an insect and succeeded, why criticize him?"

And so we turned to the text itself, the details, and the structure of the story for insights into these matters. It went on and on as we thought with the text, rather than about it, as it interrogated us, and we interrogated it. I went home and immediately wrote down as many of these stories as I could remember in my notebook on Chekhov.

Teaching at the university brought back memories of my first college English class from Professor Antonelli. I remember reading in his class Kafka's parable "Before the Law": the story about the man who waited outside the "Door of the Law" his entire life without ever passing through because he was waiting for the doorkeeper to give him permission to enter; then, just before he died, he asked the doorkeeper why nobody ever passed through the door, and the doorkeeper told him, "That's because this door was meant only for you, and now that you are dying, it's time for me to close it."

For me that door was the door to Professor Antonelli's office. I knew that if I was ever going to find myself, I was going to have to go through that door, tell him that I understood what he meant by "the inner life," and publicly declare that I wanted to be an English major—even though I knew English majors never got real jobs.

I remember the day I finally got up the courage to go to his office.

"How do you like the class so far?" he asked.

"Great," I said. "But I have to tell you that I have really only learned one thing from you this entire year."

"What's that?"

"That I am an idiot!" I said, and then looked away, my eyes burning.

"What did you expect?" he laughed. "You're only seventeen years old, and this culture *breeds* idiots. You've probably not read more than ten serious books your entire life or written more than fifty pages of serious prose. Of course you're an idiot compared to Kafka or George Eliot! But now you know what it is possible for a person to be—so *stop* being an idiot!"

He said all this with such ease, confidence, and good humor that I realized it probably wasn't an impossible aspiration.

I left his office determined to make up for lost time. I changed my major without flinching and began to read the most difficult books I could get my hands on.

But if Professor Antonelli had inspired me to work hard, it was another class that drove me further into self-examination—an advanced English composition course from Professor Werner White, a fastidious man who held high but rigid academic standards. One day, while he was passing back graded papers, one of the students interrupted him.

"Sir," he said. "There must be some mistake here. You have given me a C–."

Professor White took the paper from the young man, glanced at it, then handed it back. "No, there's no mistake Mr. Bennet, that's what the paper earned."

"But this paper is an expression of everything I know! This paper is me. Are you telling me that all I am worth is a C–?"

"No, I'm telling you that you don't know how to use the semicolon and that you don't know how to organize paragraphs."

The student got even more indignant. "Oh, so that's what this class is about, semicolons and paragraphs? It's not about honesty or truth or self-expression?"

"You've got it," Professor White replied. "I don't know what truth is, young man, but I do know what effective prose is. Look at me. I have no soul at all, and yet people tell me I am an excellent writer."

The student fell silent, sorting out Professor White's reply, and then he said, "In that case, Professor White, this paper is not a C– at all; it's an F. And an F from a man like you, sir, would be an honor. Please change my grade."

Professor White refused, and so the student stood up and ceremoniously marked an F on his own paper in large strokes and walked toward the door. But before he left, he turned to the rest of the class and said, "Who is coming with me? Are you going to let this man walk all over you?"

We were all silent. No one left with him.

"Have it your way, Sheep," he said and then bounded out of the room.

All the rest of the students, myself included, breathed a collective sigh of relief. But we also held down our heads. A part of us was with him, a part of us resented our teacher's preoccupation with formal integrity, and we longed for liberation.

The next quarter, I decided I needed to loosen up a bit, and so I took a class on the British Romantic poets from Professor Molly Miller, a sixty-two-year-old woman with long, gray hair and deep, sea-green eyes who, unlike Professor White, had a reputation as a campus radical.

The first day of class, the room was packed with over fifty students—many trying to add the course to their schedules. When Molly walked in, the class quieted down. She began by reciting Wordsworth: "My heart leaps up when I behold a rainbow in the sky. So it was when I was young, so it shall be when I am old or let me die. The child is father to the man, and I would wish my days to be bound each to each in natural piety."

No one spoke.

"Do you know what natural piety is?" she asked us. "Do you wish for it?"

Again, no one spoke.

"That is the last time I'm going to speak," she concluded. "*You* carry on."

After a long awkward silence that must have lasted at least two minutes, someone asked her if there was any room to add the course.

"Of course," she said. "I'll add until the room is full."

"How do you grade?"

"Everyone gets an A," she said. "So if you're here just for a grade, stay home. The Romantics teach us that there is nothing worse than false motives and deception."

It took the rest of the period for her to sign all the add forms, but of course, the next day of class, only six people showed up. The day after that, only three.

Molly was true to her word and didn't speak much. The discussions were dominated by a rather tiresome fellow in the front row. Molly listened politely but passively, looking around at the rest of us, as if waiting for us to speak out, wondering when someone, anyone, would assert his natural piety. I never did and stopped going to class after the third week.

Later that quarter, I was walking across campus and saw Molly coming toward me. I was trapped. I couldn't avoid her.

"Hi, Molly," I said.

"I see you've stopped coming to class," she observed.

"Yeah, well, I was going to come. Grades aren't that important to me, but that guy in the front row kept dominating the discussions."

"Whose fault is that?" she asked.

"I guess I could have said something," I admitted.

"Look," Molly said, "students will never learn anything until they take responsibility for their own educations. As long as you rely on others to motivate you or predigest things for you, you will never learn. Many of the other professors want to make you over in their image. I want to set you free. But you've got to take up the challenge and accept the responsibility."

I was too ashamed to go back to her class after that, and I know now that had I done so, it might have been one of the most important acts of my life.

My first year of graduate school, I struck up a conversation with my ethnic literature professor. He invited me to coffee, and we sat down in the school cafeteria.

"Where are you from?" he asked.

"Oh, I'm from here," I said.

"Where did you go to school as an undergraduate?" he asked, searching for something unique in my background.

"Here," I said.

I could see he wasn't satisfied.

"Inchausti, that's a Basque name, isn't it?" he asked, still searching.

"Yes, but my family is assimilated."

"Oh. . . . Do you belong to any religious or political groups?"

"No, I play baseball," I offered.

But the conversation quickly dried up, and he excused himself to do some work in his office.

I walked away a little angry at myself for being so boring and at him for having judged me so quickly. Simply because my life had been provincial and limited was no reason for him to reject me so completely. Didn't I at least possess *potential*? Wasn't I worth educating? Didn't my nothingness coupled with my eagerness to learn make me a perfect pupil? A blank page? A presence in the absence?

Besides, what was wrong with being a local boy? Certainly there was drama in that, poetry even, if one had the eyes to see. My father had a history, even if he wasn't self-consciously Basque. My mother had one too. I had friends and relatives and people who loved me. I possessed passions and secrets and dark regrets. I had a soul too, even if its qualities were not particularly pronounced.

But what were those qualities? Who was I? I had to admit I really didn't know.

In the ethnic literature class that quarter we read a host of novels by a variety of displaced souls—from the *Invisible Man* to *Barrio Boy*—and I was both awakened and reassured. Here were people who came from flat roads in backwater neighborhoods—ordinary people who struggled to find themselves, who did ordinary things and found meaning and beauty and strangeness all around them. They reached back into memories that, from another's perspective, may have seemed trivial, sectarian, or merely private to discover a life and create a self. And I could do the same if I was honest enough and brave enough to face the truth of what my experiences had made me. And my experiences had made me many things my professor could not see.

The lie was that he thought he already knew me, and like so many times before in my past when I felt misunderstood, undervalued, unfairly diminished, I turned away with a new determination to affirm myself in spite of it and with a new resolve to discover my larger self through books, ideas, and what they used to call "the great conversation."

A year later, I transferred to the University of Chicago, where I was a research assistant/boy Friday for a very famous professor who inspired me by his capacity to live, not simply profess, the life of the mind.

I'd find books in the library for him, put together bibliographies, buy potato chips for his dinner parties, and drive assorted luminaries to and from his home.

One night, my job was to drive a famous literary critic from the lecture hall to my professor's house for a dinner party and then drive my professor's cook home. When I came to pick up his cook, the guests were applauding her wonderful cuisine. She was a black woman in her sixties, and she smiled and accepted their applause graciously. Then she walked up to the critic—herself a woman in her sixties—and admired her earrings.

"My, my, those are wonderful earrings. I bet they are very expensive. My, my, they are so beautiful."

I wondered if she was being polite or making some sort of oblique social commentary. It was hard to say.

I told her I was there to drive her home.

"No, no, Sonny, no need to drive me home. I'll just take the bus . . . although the other night, those boys did bother me."

I got the distinct impression this time that she *was* making social commentary.

"Come on," I said. "Tell me how to get to your house."

It wasn't a long drive, maybe ten minutes through some very ominous urban territory.

She made small talk on the way, talking about crime and the dangers of riding city buses.

When I dropped her off, I could see the curtain part in the window on the second floor and a small child's head duck back inside.

After she got out of the car and safely into her home, I locked the car door on her side and drove quickly back to my professor's house.

I felt vaguely unsettled. Why did she have so little when others had so much? Did it make sense for me to return to my residence hall to write a paper on Wallace Stevens so that someday I could be a professor when right before my eyes hardworking women had been cut off from such possibilities? St. Francis would have given the woman his coat. No, he would have given the woman the professor's car, dropped out of graduate school, and lived a life of service in the streets.

But I didn't do that. I went back to my room and started typing away. "The only emperor is the emperor of ice cream."

But what did I know about emperors? What did I know about melting? I suddenly felt sheltered, protected, unreal. I wanted to call my professor and ask him, "How can we live with it? The injustices? Our comforts? Beautiful lives amid such struggle? How could Wallace Stevens, an insurance executive, dare to call himself a 'connoisseur of chaos'? And how dare I claim that I understood him?"

I was very young then, and when I went to bed that night, cuddled up in those clean dorm linens, no doubt washed and pressed by other black women, I muttered the line from Chekhov's "Gooseberries": "Lord, forgive us sinners!"

I wouldn't say this was one of the defining moments of my life. We have all had many like it. Sudden and startling, momentary pangs of conscience.

What is one to do with them? What are they telling us? Live responsibly? But how? Don't forget the excluded? But is memory enough?

Brother Blake helped me to see what my professor probably would have told me had I asked him—that such moments meant for me to *become a teacher.* Not become a successful professional, but a *teacher*, someone who takes up his very life into speech so that others might do the same.

But did I have the resources? Could I tell the stories? Could I own up to what life had made of me? Could I enact the poem of the mind, finding what will suffice? Could I be *that* honest?

It wasn't really a choice any longer; it was the only way left open to me. And I would serve it forever in total obedience to its mysteries without ever looking back.

14

Program Notes

Mankind is always advancing, and man always remains the same.

Goethe

The higher Enthusiasm of man's nature is for the while without Exponent; yet it continues indestructible, unweariedly active and works blindly in the great chaotic deep.

Thomas Carlyle

June

To survive as a teacher, one must master the art of creative suffering. Like Gandhi's nonviolent soldiers of truth, the dedicated teacher must walk into the assault of pettiness and disinterest every day with no expectation of victory—serene only in the hope that the abuse one endures is redemptive and encouraged by the conviction that teaching is, above all other things, an art of endurance.

Elie Wiesel tells the story of the rabbi who, as a young man, wanted to change the world with his preaching. Every day he would mount his soapbox, denounce the untransformed world, and chart the path to salvation. He did this for many years, and the world did not change. In fact, things only got worse. And yet, every day he proclaimed his message.

When he became an old man, someone said to him, "Rabbi, you have been proclaiming God for over fifty years and nothing has changed. Why don't you just give up?"

And the rabbi said, "Yes, it is true. When I was young, I preached because I thought I could change the world. But I don't preach for that reason anymore. Today I preach so that the world does not change me."

Here is a vision of the teacher—not as a change agent, social worker, or therapist, but as prophetic exception.

And so the issue for beginning teachers is not how the posturing and defensiveness of their students can be overcome by creative appeals to their own sense of self-interest, but how such defensiveness can be endured and thereby transformed into a power for the good.

One of the greatest films dramatizing the art of teaching is Arthur Penn's adaptation of William Gibson's play *The Miracle Worker.* The climactic water pump scene alone tells us almost everything we need to know about what it means to teach students who are convinced that we have nothing to teach them.

Annie Sullivan is sitting at the family dinner table, celebrating Helen Keller's return to the family home after living in isolation with Annie for two weeks of intense language training. Helen's father, a traditional Victorian patriarch, is ecstatic because Annie has succeeded in teaching the girl table manners. But Annie is frustrated because the child still hasn't grasped the fundamental symbolic connection between signs and things, between language and reality. She still cannot think.

To see if the rigorous discipline established over the past two weeks still applies in her parents' home, Helen begins to "forget" her manners and willfully drops her napkin. The mother wishes to let this indiscretion go uncorrected, but Annie demands that Helen pick it up.

In defiance, Helen sweeps her arm across the table, smashing the china and sending her mother's roast flying across the room. She then takes a pitcher of water and splashes it in Annie's face.

Realizing that everything is at stake here, Annie picks Helen up, carries her outside, and makes her refill the pitcher at the water pump. As she does so, Annie begins, for what seems like the millionth time, to sign words into Helen's hand and then place in Helen's hands the signed objects.

"Pump," Annie says, and thrusting Helen's hands to the pump handle, she signs, "P-U-M-P."

"Pitcher," she says, and clasping Helen's hands around the pitcher, she signs, "P-I-T-C-H-E-R."

It is clear that Annie is doing this not because she thinks Helen will learn this time, but simply because she doesn't know what else to do. Helen resists—crying, kicking, pushing, and pulling.

Then, as instantly as this outburst had begun, Helen's tantrum stops. She becomes quiet, absorbed, perfectly still. Rapt with attention, Helen finally makes the connection between words and things, signs and experience, and for the first time in her life, she understands an abstraction. In that glorious scene, Helen says, "Wa, wa."

In a moment, her world is transformed.

But what happens next is every bit as moving.

Helen whirls around the yard trying to touch EVERYTHING, thirsty for the signs to say her world. "What's this?" Helen indicates, touching a post, "and this? And this? And this?" Annie calls to the parents: "Mr. and Mrs. Keller! Come! Come! Helen knows. She KNOWS!"

Helen's parents emerge from the dining room, and Helen runs to embrace them—touching their faces and signing their names, knowing them, in a way, for the very first time. But then she stops, walks over to Annie Sullivan, and touches her face.

Annie signs out the word "T-E-A-C-H-E-R." And they embrace. It is what one might call a messianic moment, for it is clear that from now on, Annie and Helen will share an intimacy far deeper than mere sentiment. Annie is not a parent, limited by pity or frustrated by libidinal bonds. She is something different, something much more profound, something awesome and holy. She is a *teacher*, an ally to the heroic possibilities within, what William Gibson calls, "a miracle worker."

This inspiring vision of the teacher as pragmatic prophet parallels many of my own experiences with great teachers. Had I not met a certain dedicated and uncompromising professor my sophomore year at the state university, I might very well have lost my soul. Had he not placed my hand upon the works of William Blake and made the signs of life, and had he not persisted in making those signs after I shrugged him off, placing my hands again on the novels of Dostoyevsky, and then again on the essays of Emerson, I would never have heard the call. But thanks to my teacher I, like Helen, was obligated now both to live this higher existence and to pass it along.

The question was how? How was I to connect my sense of vocation to the largely indifferent world in which I found myself immersed? It was as if, in waking up to the fact that the world had yet to be fully discovered or honestly described, I had not been liberated at all, but rather infected with an incurable disease that forever severed me from my world.

This lack of continuity between my inner life and outer circumstances baffled me for many years. I knew I was called to the life of the mind, but it seemed that the life of the mind had no place to lay its head. It didn't really seem welcome in the schools I had attended or affirmed by the television shows I watched or by the jobs I held or even by the career ambitions I was encouraged to adopt. I found it reflected only in the artistic and religious extremes—in the literary masters and mystics, in plebeian reformers and philosophical outcasts.

This bothered me, for what good was an exalted sense of human possibility if it only alienated you from a society that operated on much less sublime premises? What good were precise articulations of contemporary dilemmas if one's leaders and institutions were simply too coarse or too distant to register them? And what did eloquence matter if nature herself absorbed all of our protests into an abyss of sex, death, and indifference?

Such were the preoccupations of my postadolescent search for meaning, and these themes have, more or less, preoccupied me ever since. It was only through Brother Blake that I was ever able to resolve them. No, not resolve them, but to see them as the themes and preoccupations of a great vocation: the way of the classroom teacher.

The news in my mailbox contained a dittoed announcement from Strapp explaining that the humanities program was being eliminated and replaced by more "traditional" English and history courses. The interdisciplinary experiment was over. Full details would be provided later.

I was not surprised, but finding the message like that in my box, on that damned, smudged ditto paper, was insulting. It was as if someone had, in an offhanded way, just annulled my baptism.

I read it again just to make sure. My stomach turned. It was true.

I sought out Mike Morton to ease my despair.

"This decision was probably made months ago," he said. "Maybe last year. They waited until now to tell us because they didn't have time to institute a new program, and they didn't want you new guys feeling like lame ducks your first year. They have probably already ordered the books."

"Don't we get any say in this?" I asked.

"Sure, we are the ones who have got to figure out how to teach the new curriculum. It will be lots of fun. There'll be lots of meetings."

And with that, he was off to get some coffee.

I called Linda to tell her the news and seek some consolation. She told me to talk to Brother Blake.

It was early, just after seven A.M., still cold and foggy. You could barely see twenty feet across the football field. I found Brother Blake out on the track, taking his morning constitutional with Brother Arnold. He was as happy and as chipper as I'd ever seen him.

"Did you hear about the humanities program?" I asked him.

"Oh, yes. Last night. They like to change things," he said.

"But we can't let them," I said. "I mean, this program is *so* fine."

"It's never the program," he said. "It's the teacher. Don't worry. Nothing of importance can be touched by those guys. They just want to be able to sell something new to the parents. They change things around every five years. Real education is beyond them, out of their hands. Our battleground is the classroom, not the curriculum."

"But aren't they the same thing?" I asked.

"Hardly," he said. "You know yourself that you could teach these kids Buddhism from the first grade, and the majority of them would still want careers in show business. The most we can do is teach them how to learn, not what to know. The administrators don't understand this. They keep making curriculum changes, but they never really get what it is we do. It's not the natural man we serve, but the divine light."

Then he and Brother Arnold, never having stopped walking, magically disappeared into the fog, leaving me standing there.

As an afterthought, Brother Blake shouted back out of the mist, "They can't even see us!"

I could hear him and Brother Arnold chuckling at the pun.

I ran after him and grasped his arm, my forehead wet with sweat and fog. I didn't know quite what to say, so I just blurted out, "Brother Blake, how can I thank you?"

"Thank yourself," he said. "I never gave you anything. You took it. Thank yourself for recognizing that I had something worth taking."

It seemed silly somehow to have found such powerful truths in such a withered body and in such a provincial place. But I had found them there, and who was I to refuse the revelation? If Brother Blake was not bothered by the curriculum changes, I figured, why should I be? The sublime pedagogy would continue one by one, soul by soul, connection by connection, regardless of the textbooks or the grading system—maybe even in spite of them.

Classroom teaching is a great existential art, if we would only own up to what a serious and difficult craft it really is. The best teachers know this; that's what makes them the best teachers. But beginning teachers have to be reminded that their vocation is sublime—bigger than they know, bigger than anyone knows. And though there will be times when the pettiness of one's circumstances seems overwhelming, those circumstances are the very stuff of self-creation. And so, even though pettiness cannot be overcome, even though it manifests itself as a trap and a prison, it *can* be reflected upon and understood—transformed into lesson and parable by the thinking heart. I knew this perspective meant trouble for me, that it sealed within me difficult obligations that it would be much easier to live without. And yet, these obligations created in me a new center of identity and a willingness to pursue a delayed but difficult reward.

What scared me was that my perceptions seemed to operate now in *unseen worlds*.

The graduation was held in the gym. Rows of folding chairs, oak podium, flowers, and formality.

There would be no troubling Zen Koans from Brother Blake to decipher today. Brother Nep was the main speaker. He didn't wear his Greek sailor's cap tonight. He was in formal Brothers' robes.

"We are here today," he intoned, clearly enjoying the resonance of his voice, "to mark an inward occasion with an outward sign, to participate in ritual and communion, to mark a graduation, a turning, a step along life's path."

BLAM! BLAM! BLAM!

Suddenly, firecrackers exploded at Brother Nep's feet. The seniors had tossed them up on the stage from the front row.

"Well, look at the spirit of these boys," Nep continued. "Energy and ambition beyond bounds, exploding before us."

The audience laughed. Strapp was taking down names.

Behind me, one of the mothers saw nothing but her child. She was smiling, but tears were running down her cheeks.

"There he is," she told her husband, "just in front of the principal in the first row."

And as she got out her camera, I understood that this ritual would survive Brother Nep's web-spinning and several packets of firecrackers. It was as if, in seeing the end of high school, I had at last grasped its beginning and knew the place for the first time.

We are powered by larger forces than we can comprehend, and as teachers, we serve our individual students' quests to make sense of it all—not by re-creating them in our image, but by throwing light on their lives as they go zooming past.

Brother Charlie showed slides of the graduating seniors using the same machine he had used at Brother Bob's funeral—the one that let one image fade into the next. There were shots of boys eating lunch, playing football, close-ups of their faces and eyes, smiles, and personalities. All the while, a song by the Moody Blues was playing in the background, a song about time moving like a river and flowing to the sea—no doubt a rip-off of some ancient Celtic dirge, but it was still effective, its theme poignant: Will we ever meet again?

I was moved but hated the fact that Brother Charlie's cinematic tricks were moving me. I resisted, resented, and tried to get cynical. But the slides were so beautiful, the music so sentimental, and the tears in the mothers' eyes so true, I got a lump in my throat anyway.

A vocation is not a single narrative: it is a perpetually improvised dialogue. You can't know it like you know your part in a play or your position on a team. You know it the way that you know you have heard enough or that you have been down too long. You know it once or twice in a profound life-shattering way, but you know it again many times later as a refinement of purpose in a moment of despair, as a shift in attention or concern, or as the birth of a new perception or insight.

I knew I no longer needed St. Vincent's or Brother Blake to teach me these things. I didn't need the humanities program or anything else. One found one's community in those who struggled against the will-lessness of the common, everyday round—in those who fought against the comfortable and merely workable, and in those who longed for the good.

There are many ways to teach successfully, but there is only one pedagogy of the sublime. This prophetic art is born of poetry, excess, exaggeration, and risk. It is not so much a means of instruction as it is a call to self-transcendence, an act of liberation, a pure expenditure of energy in an excess of shame. And one can only learn how to do it the same way Kafka learned how to write—out of a marriage of desperation and infinite longing.

This kind of education operates outside the cult of professional efficiency. It is an anti-technique powered by metaphor, irony, and a profound skepticism toward the ways of the world. And because its revelations emerge only to solitary individuals, it cannot be rigorously defined. It can only be experienced and described, like the fragrance of mangoes or the view from the top of Mt. Etna.

The pedagogies taught in our schools of education too often have far less exalted ambitions. They seek to pass on skills, efficiency, and social power—to prepare students for college or law school or the state plumbing-certificate exam. They are *not* prophetic or philosophic, but agents of the marketplace—instrumental, reductive, and finally despiriting.

Many beginning teachers find themselves caught between these two visions of education. Intuitively, they sense that the prophetic art is the higher calling, that their students need someone to bless their budding inwardness and longing to transcend. But the schools are often set up to do just the reverse: infect their students with worldly ambitions. And so, during their first years, a battle often wages inside the souls of young teachers as to whether they are going to try to set their young students free by practicing the pedagogy of the sublime (which may take them many painful years to master and even then never conclusively) or adopt coping strategies that will allow them to fulfill their professional agenda and survive the daily round.

Most accede to professionalism out of psychological necessity. The way of the teacher as liberator is simply too difficult.

Besides, the sheer magnitude of their everyday responsibilities compels them to lower their ambitions. Without the encouragement of administrators or colleagues like Brother Blake, beginning teachers simply lack the courage to take upon themselves the risk of forging their own original approaches in the classroom. So they lean upon the props of conventional practice, three-step lesson plans, and programmed textbooks. As a result, they do not dive into the abyss of authentic student-teacher relations to discover for themselves the truth of Nietzsche's maxim that out of chaos comes order.

And yet, despite the risks, the pains, and the lack of guidance, a few teachers, like Brother Blake, still take the plunge. These "true educators" often attribute their powers to the particular subject matters they teach—history, mathematics, philosophy, biology. And yet, it is clear to anyone who knows them that their craft *as teachers* is separate from their knowledge as scholars— higher, hidden, more difficult to discern. These teachers *know* something that the others do not. They have risked more; they have ventured further. They have explored more fully the links between their discipline and the inner life, and so their students listen to them differently, more seriously, as if with some sixth sense.

Brother Blake taught me how to connect with this sixth sense. And I was so grateful that I wrote down virtually every word he ever spoke to me. They are the contents of this book.

Maxims, Aphorisms, Insights, and Reflections on the Art of Classroom Teaching, by Brother Blake

Begin each day by telling yourself: Today I shall be meeting with interference, ingratitude, insolence, disloyalty, ill will and selfishness—all of them due to the offender's ignorance of what is good or evil. But for my part I have long perceived the nature of good and its nobility; . . . therefore none of these things can injure me, for nobody can implicate me in what is degrading.

Marcus Aurelius, Meditations

• It is a terrifying thought to think of our classrooms as laboratories for self-creation and existential discovery. How could anybody administer that? But that is exactly what they are! And so the teacher's lessons are never separate from the teacher's own evolving intellectual identity.

• When you talk to your ninth grade class, talk to yourself as if your ninth grade self was in the room—only smarter, more perceptive, less emotionally bound. What did you need to hear? What would have captured your attention? What would have set you free? This approach works, not because our students are just like we were, but because kids at this age cannot imagine their own lives in any historical context, so you must do it for them—only generously, honestly, perceptively.

• If you stop observing, you're finished. But you don't have to do this consciously, except maybe at the beginning. Everything you see, both inside and outside of class, goes into the bank of your awareness and will emerge in time, as needed, if you attend to the business of witnessing to the truths before you. Teaching, in this sense, is a mysterious process. The mind begins to function in a different way, making odd new connections, until lessons emerge of their own accord out of the environment, like leaves from a tree.

• The way I teach difficult material is simply to assume from the outset that none of them are going to follow me anyway, so who cares?

• The essence of teaching, the soul of the art, is being brave enough, psychologically unencumbered enough, to see exactly what is taking place in the minds of your students at any given moment and then—like a good psychotherapist—speak to and through their defenses to uncover the true promise of the lesson, its hidden meaning. This significance, of course, will almost always be different from what you originally took it to be, and it is usually at odds with the lesson plan. But that is what makes teaching a creative act! One doesn't just dispense knowledge—one brings it into being. I am surprised by what I "teach" all the time!

• Teachers have to learn to respond to all the intellectual dangers and possibilities emerging around them as their lessons proceed. And if they are good enough, and they get lucky, their responses will sometimes mesh with the truth of the moment, and an authentic insight is powerfully communicated to their students. It might not be the teacher's original insight; it seldom is. It might be Newton's or Tolstoy's—but the teacher somehow connects up with it in her voice or in her gestures or even in her silences, and the idea comes alive; it's worth rendered both obvious and profound.

More often than not, however, the teacher's words both hit and miss simultaneously. A few students connect, others do not. A metaphor works—but not exactly. And so choices have to be made on the spot, thoughts recast, the teacher's reading of the moment reassessed. All of this "give" makes teaching an art where one is constantly acquiring new skills and responsibilities.

• Nothing happens until somebody comes along. A teacher is somebody who *comes along*.

• Teachers need not outline great amounts of material. Textbooks do that far more efficiently. Teachers are there to provide perspective. To relate the part to the whole, to link the discipline to the student's life, to connect the passion to the prose.

• I once had a student come to me and ask me what he had to do to get an A in my class.

"I'll do anything!" he said.

So I said, "Okay, run through that wall over there, and when you are done, run through this wall here."

Well, he tried. He bounced off each wall in a mock effort to do whatever had to be done to get an A.

And I said, "Well, now I have to give you an F."

"Why?" he asked incredulously.

"Because the first lesson in the humanities is not to do stupid things just because someone in authority tells you to do them."

• Poets are tempted to destroy language in order to create their own, but novelists are different. They don't have the temptation to destroy language per se, so much as to destroy history, truth, common sense—in order to create a new history, a new truth, and a new common sense. Teachers are closer to novelists than to poets. They are masters of the unreality of the actual and fascinated by the wisdom of exaggeration.

• To be a truly logical thinker, one must be willing to entertain nihilism or at least adopt the role of the nihilist—believing nothing, trusting no one. People with faith are less willing to do this than people without faith, and people with hope less willing to do this than people without hope, and so, by default, the worst among us end up defining what's rational.

• A teacher has not started teaching until she can rise above the narrow concerns of her particular class and curriculum to the broader issues of her discipline and its relationship to her times.

• Just as all art today is "conceptual art," no matter what it may call itself, all instruction today is theater, no matter what anyone says. To teach without theatrical considerations is to become dramatic in spite of yourself. That is to say, to become parody!

• A good lecture-discussion consists in the painting of the mind into corners, followed by a series of miraculous escapes and rescues.

• Teaching—like drama—is an act of pure presence in imaginary time. All delays are overcome in the instant, and it gives us the sense that, at least for the space of one class period, we actually exist.

• I once taught a Virginia Woolf novel at the seminary to the novices. I put a chart of all the characters on the board along with a time line of all the events that took place in the novel.

One of my brightest students raised an important objection. "Doesn't placing all of these materials in charts on the board violate Virginia Woolf's intentions as a novelist? Doesn't she want us to experience the overlapping, multidimensional nature of experience that defies logical categorization?"

"That is true," I replied. "But class lectures don't take place in the real time of experience; they take place in the imaginary time of pure presence. When you walk through that classroom door, time stops. And so we can put up on the board structures obscured by the flow of events. When class is over, you will enter real time again. You will read the novel on its own terms, and these charts and time lines will remain in your memory merely as a dream to make sense of the novel as it flies by."

• It is not how much you know, but in what context it is retained and used. This is the essence of talent—the ability to translate, adapt, and refine ideas in the moment as needed. It is grace under pressure, the courage that is authentic thought. We serve our students most when we can demonstrate this value to them.

• A teacher should avoid explaining things. Explanations undermine complexity. Replace them with stories or questions, anything that keeps irony alive. We shouldn't solve problems so much as turn them into significant occasions.

• High-minded teachers keep the dream of a better life alive in the young. And even if you feel unworthy when they project their ideals upon you, remember that there are larger forces at play than your ordinary self. As a teacher, you become a mirror and an icon of their best selves, so let them use you in this way. Just don't ever believe that you *are* your teacherly function.

• One must come to literature from experience, not to experience from literature.

• These kids must be awakened to their terrible beauty.

• You can tell the quality of your lesson by the looks on your students' faces. When you present ideas in the right way, their faces change. They get alert, they listen, they respond more openly, they laugh more easily, they are explorative, likable. But when you appeal to their fears or ambitions, right away they get rigid, defensive, proud, unhappy, and anxious.

• Beginning teachers often underestimate the value of endurance as a lesson in itself. If you fail to inspire your students day after day but continue trying to teach them anyway, eventually, some of them will ask themselves, "What does this guy think he's got that he keeps coming at us day after day?" And then they will ask you and even listen closely to your answer. That's the day you had better be good. They'll give even the most abject loser "one day" to show his stuff, if he persists.

But even if you blow that one day, keep coming at them, and your endurance and conviction will earn you another day, and another, until after a while, your entire year is punctuated by "holidays" of authentic conversations.

• People become teachers for the same reasons people become novelists: out of desperation. But the desperation is a little different in each case. Writing a novel is often a last-ditch effort at making one's life significant. A teaching career often begins as a search for meaningful employment. Novelists are driven by a metaphysical quest, teachers by an untapped energy.

• Some students want you to grade them on their relationship to you as a person. You've got to confront this. Make it clear to them that you grade their work the way a poultry man grades eggs or a butcher grades meat. Too many spots, too little muscle, too much fat, and the work is not grade A prime—no matter how wonderful the steer who gave his life to produce it. Just as there are market standards for meat, so too are there market standards for term papers and tests. Grades just make it clear how to apply the conventional criteria—no more and no less. Students should learn not to take them personally.

• Yeats once said that a man may not know the truth, but he might be able to embody it. Teachers neither know the truth nor do they embody it. For them, truth is like water forever slipping through their fingers. Their only artistry, their only expertise, is that sometimes they remember to cup their hands.

• Teaching, like coaching, is often a matter of speaking the same inner language as your students. That's why administrators place so much hope in finding teachers of the same race, class, and sex as their students. They hope that they can speak the same inner language. But it's not that easy, because coming from the same cultural background does not guarantee that one speaks any "inner language" at all.

• The trick in sports is learning how to forget about the competition and concentrate on running your own race. You've got to focus on the dynamics of the ball in flight, not on the personality or motivations of the pitcher who threw it. When I was young, I was a "thinking" player. But it is far better to be a "thoughtless" one, or should I say "feeling" one, so present to the realities of the moment that you simply act in harmony with the flow of the game.

This is a hard lesson for young athletes to learn, because as spectators, they are encouraged to adopt exactly the opposite interests. They are thrilled by the drama of things, the personalities of the players, the social context within which the game is occurring, even its place in sports history. But inside the game, these interests are vices—distractions. Athletes concentrate on specifics, on craft. Was it Ezra Pound who said, "I judge a man's sincerity by the quality of his technique"? Well, whoever said that was a *player.*

• Many students, like good deconstructionists, spend a lot of time searching for the thread that unties the lesson: the grading criteria, the hidden fetish, what they take to be the real course content. And the teacher, if he is any good, frustrates their bad faith by constantly returning to the mystery of his subject matter.

It is not a matter of techniques or tricks; it is a matter of eluding the students' traps, their nets of definitions, their desire to turn off the dialogue by finding the certainty, the bias, the lie at the heart of the teacherly myth.

• Nothing said in class means the same thing as if it were said in common conversation. The classroom changes the nature of language, making it useless for everyday use but supercharged with a value one might very well call "novelistic" were its ironies not so much more unstable.

• Teaching is a performance in language, so when you speak in class, you cannot just talk like a normal person. Or rather, when you do, you have got to be in on the joke that everything being said is part of a play of invented selves and so bracketed as existing in a universe that is the psychological counterpoint to reality—but not reality itself.

• Many students sense that their teachers hold to values that are in cultural retreat and so withhold their allegiance to them out of a false sense of self-preservation. To undo this reticence is, in some sense, the teacher's calling.

• The classroom is a mirror of the self and a window into the future. It mirrors the self in our feelings about it. The students embody all our unconscious traits, and when we can't stand them, we can be sure that an ugly part of ourselves has just been revealed to us and that we are being challenged to own up to some hypocrisy or self-deceit. We are being asked to free up some of the energy we have attached to keeping hold of our own grandiose images of ourselves.

• The key to effective lecturing is to have a purpose, not a message. If your mind is occupied with your purpose, it finds messages to fulfill it, images and examples born of objects and incidents in the room and memories to support your points. This is the key to thinking on your feet and responding to the students' questions and comments. Fulfilling your purpose—to inspire and to reveal, not just passing on information—this is putting cause before effect.

• So often, teachers confuse getting depressed with achieving humility, but real humility comes from seeing how little it is that you actually know and then proceeding to do something about it.

• When we look at students, we see through them into our pasts. But when they look at us, they see through us into their futures. Both acts of the imagination are fraught with the dangers of inflation and distortion. And yet, it's important to know that very little of what takes place in the classroom takes place in the present. The classroom is the zone of imagination—a place of mind, not of fact.

• To take up the possibility of becoming a teacher, one must first take up the responsibility of being a human being. Expertise and professional training can never replace the power of possessing a world view.

• I always have trouble designing tests. The students learn more in my class in fifteen minutes than I would ever have the time to test them on: insights without end, images that reverberate throughout a lifetime, calls to transcend and transcend again, scientific theories whose full implications they may never ultimately grasp. I am not trying to sound arrogant; it's just that our curriculum really is sublime.

• Brother Blake had a quote from Robert Coles (taken from one of Jonathan Kozol's books) pinned up beside his desk: "In this life we prepare for things, for moments and events and situations. . . . We worry about wrongs, think about injustices, read what Tolstoi or Ruskin . . . has to say. . . . Then all of a sudden, the issue is not whether we agree with what we have heard and read and studied. . . . The issue is *us*, and what we have become."

• Almost always, the most popular teachers are the worst. They are popular because they make thought easy and accessible; they model a kind of intellectual efficiency that is, at bottom, antithetical to real thought. Efficient teachers are, by definition, antiphilosophical.

• Students often feel that they are making great sacrifices to understand us, and we should not belittle what they take to be—however misguided—their own authentic generosity.

• Talking to students outside of class, one can be onself. That is to say, one can wear a mask! But in class, one must use all of one's talents to achieve an authentic speech. The fact that one ends up creating personae anyway need not discourage us, for these selves are dummy selves, props in the search for reality, and the students know that and grant us that conceit.

• The best teachers are not those who amaze us with their eloquence or arrest our imaginations with their brilliance or even get us to work without our noticing it. They are those who reveal some realm of existence previously unknown to us and thereby redeem us from our forgetfulness and lost sublimity.

• Those who believe that it is the purpose of the teacher to impart knowledge fail to see that the domain of the classroom teacher is not the unknown, but the forgotten. Human existence is perpetually being forgotten, insights mislaid, whole civilizations lost, and teaching is the only way through which they can be recovered. We don't create knowledge, we reanimate it. This is why the best teacherly discourse is poetic, metaphoric, but not, strictly speaking, aesthetic.

• You've got to learn to read your students like characters in a Chekhov play—not by their outward appearances, but by their emotional preoccupations. What is fascinating about them is not their ages or their times, not their clothes or their fads, but their feeling life—and that is something secret and often hidden, even from themselves. In conversation, you can sometimes bring it out. In their papers, it will sometimes come through.

• A student is not merely a human resource. A student is a person, and a person is a story.

• A teacher is finally someone who can communicate what it *feels like* to know difficult things. Students who have experienced the power of ideas in this way are infected with intellectual desire—which is something other than curiosity about the way the world works. It is deeper, more profound; it is a longing not just *to know things*, but to fully understand and assimilate the significance of what one *does know*. It is a hunger for meaning and for firsthand, personal experience of the good.

• Culture exists, not only to keep alive the fresh flow of ideas, but also to keep alive a certain level of sensitivity, a degree of intellectual focus, and the will to a precise use of language. After reading Rilke, for instance, I turn back to my world, and everything seems coarse, ungainly, lacking in precise distinctions. My own inner life compared to the jewel-like sensibility of the poet seems splattered and flooded, without significant form, and I am forced to face the message of the Torso of Apollo: "You must change your life." This is the way students should feel when they leave our classrooms: that they are leaving a golden room where honesty, subtlety, truth, and precision give form to their deepest sense of themselves. And even though many of them will feel those values evaporate into "life" the minute they walk out the door, a residue will remain to be tapped again somewhere else.

• The more you know about a subject, the harder it is to teach it, because you replace the energy of discovery born of risk and error with the deadening surety of statement and expertise. As the teacher gets out ahead of his students, they get left behind—feel

depressed, overwhelmed. "He's way out there," they say to themselves, "and I'm still trying to get this basic stuff!"

• Statements are especially tricky, because they exclude as much
as they include. As a rule, you should avoid making them, but when
you do, it should be done with conviction, and it should be a
pronouncement—a summing up.

• We are not the transmitters of a tradition, but workers in a
philosophy coming into existence of which "the tradition" is one
very important part.

• Teachers must not be afraid of being philosophers, or they will
forfeit their functions as prophets and fools.

• The history of "The Sublime Pedagogy" is hidden, because it
is disguised as poetics. In other words, all education of the spirit
is indirect. It has to be. The soul is shy, like a deer, and can't be
approached straight-on. Poetics is the "science" of indirection. Its
essence is metaphor, irony, myth—the arts of the tangential. Once
you turn teaching into a method with precise definitions and a rigid
game plan, you kill it, because you eliminate the "give" inherent
in poetic language. You destroy the space within the words where
individuals can find themselves. You build edifices of meaning,
beautiful, great skyscrapers of relationships, but the deer disappear
into the underbrush.

• I am close to seventy years old, and yet even now, when I face
my classes, I sometimes have feelings of utter helplessness. I start
a discussion, retell a lecture, start a unit, but I know it hasn't been
real, and so I have to go home and feel the energy again somehow.
Usually I read a passage from Henry James and it inspires me. It
reminds me that someone else dedicated his life to trying to express
the invisible realty we all live in, and I realize that I am not alone,
that if James attempted it, it cannot be futile, and I am ready to
begin again.

• When you get older, you do not necessarily get wiser, but you
do get stories. I guess the trick of growing old gracefully is learning
how not to bore people with them. Staying young psychologically

is really about becoming a good storyteller. Taking all those stories and turning them into fresh insights. "Old" people tend to moralize, turn their stories into parables of self-justification—or worse, "proofs" of their own increasingly rigid principles. I've tried to resist that by embracing the ironies and paradoxes of my life. Literature teaches us how to stay young!

• I find it often takes two days to teach a single lesson: one day to mis-teach it, another to correct and transform the original misconception. Beginning teachers don't know this. They always want to do everything right the first time, and it just doesn't work that way. Often, the very best lessons are born of second thoughts, revisions, qualification.

• A person who never experiments in the classroom never finds out that all the old things are true.

• If you are concerned with achieving some specific result, you lose your nerve. You start getting angry, impatient, take shortcuts. You try this, you try that, you never remain faithful to any long-term strategy. But if you can get yourself to give up on success—that is, give up on the success of getting the students to see things *correctly*—you become centered, and this allows you to acquire the peace and poise you need to make discoveries in the moment.

• A teacher is not impressed by her own ideas. She explores them. She feels her way in classroom discussions in an effort to reveal some unknown aspect of the subject matter under investigation. She is not interested in her own voice, but in the form the dialogue with her students seems to be seeking, and only those forms that link the lesson to the life she shares with her students become a part of her work. Such "work" is radically ephemeral, but it's what we do.

• The only context for the evaluation of a teacher's work is the history of the dialogic imagination. The teacher need answer only to Socrates.

• Some teachers play the buffoon or the clown in order to make points and protect themselves from their students. This can work for a while. The problem is that the mask may stick, and pretty soon you find yourself stuck in the role of an eccentric, and you begin to have problems at home and outside of class. You become a crank with a huge mustache!

• We are given freedom so that we can learn we do not need it. Take freedom away, and no one can serve. That's the doctrine of free will in a nutshell.

• One day, I forgot to erase the blackboard before my seventh period class, so I just pulled down the world map to cover all the notes from the sixth period class's discussion. As the seventh period class discussed the book, I noticed they were saying all the same things the sixth period had said. So I let them talk and talk until someone said, "Don't you think we should be writing this stuff down?"

And I said, "I already have!" Then I stepped back and lifted the map to reveal a list of every single point they had made—including some they were just about to make! They thought it was magic! They thought I was a clairvoyant!

"How did you do that?" they asked.

I told them that just because their ideas *feel* new doesn't mean that they are original. We've done a good job of relearning all the old truths and stating the obvious; now let's venture into the unknown.

• A school is not an institution for the training of young minds so much as a living laboratory in philosophic anthropology. That's what Plato's academy was, that's what the Lyceum was, and that's what American high schools still are, in spite of themselves.

• There is a difference between being a teacher and being a friend. Friends pass in and out of one another like air; teachers stick, resist, a part of them always remains unabsorbed and "difficult."

• The idea of the teacher must not be defined but left open, shifting, ever in flux. One can't let one's image of what it is one is doing in the classroom become an attitude or an identity or a profession. Your identity and sense of definition must change constantly as the body changes, as the body politic changes, as the walls of one's classroom implode or expand.

• There can be no political education per se. Education is personal and against any and all repressions of the truth. Political education is a limiting of the subject matter and, therefore, implies some sort of compromise with one's body, with one's dreams and desires. True education is a constant re-creation of fresh visions of the totality of human possibility via acts of bravery and sublime articulation. It is inevitably political, but it is not consciousness-raising.

• For the ancient Greeks, education was preparation for leadership, that meant learning how to respond creatively to chaos and crisis and learning how to take responsibility and stand for values greater than oneself. Odysseus, Oedipus, Socrates—all of these figures model this turn of mind. But it is hard for us to communicate this to our students when there is no one in their experience who models these values. So when we ask them to read these ancient texts, it is almost as if we are asking them to fantasize a kind of being for which there are no recognizable human correlates. That is why I so shamelessly make connections between the action in the novels and the events of everyday life, constantly crossing the border between the imaginary and the real, between historical figures and mythic ones, between actual history and unlikely possibilities. It is the only way to educate the imagination.

• Just seeing the reality before us, registering its paradoxes and contradictions, is a great achievement and pays off in subtle ways we may not consciously realize. It is important to see what is taking place in the classroom, even if one is helpless to change it. *Especially* if one is helpless to change it! For, in the seeing, a kind of emotional distancing and sorting takes place that makes possible new avenues of engagement. Just noticing the chaos is the first step toward discerning a pattern. And when the pattern emerges—that is to say, when the unique character of an event stands revealed—then an imperative emerges, and you know what you must do.

But you have to wait for the pattern to emerge; you can't force it. This kind of thinking is not so much a matter of intelligence or clever problem solving as it is a courageous attention to particulars and the patience to wait for an authentic revelation. It cannot be reduced to a technique, since it can only be acquired through bravery.

• Stand up for the boy and show him that his desires for heroism—up to now imaginary—can become a creative reality.

• Christ does not command; he calls us to him. He does not guide; he attracts.

• Beginning classroom teachers, like new stepparents, find themselves caught inside an odd dynamic. The kind of authority I had over my students, formal and punitive, was not the kind I wanted. And the kind of authority I wanted, informal existential authority, is very difficult to get. And so, as a new teacher I existed in a psychological limbo—perpetually unsure as to my exact role and status. I felt both too powerful and not powerful enough at the same time, like a rebel who woke up to find himself emperor of a realm he had spent his life trying to destroy.

• People with weak egos are tempted to become teachers, because they think having power over others will make their egos strong—having institutional authority gives them the illusion of self-mastery. And so, in time, they become petty tyrants and pass on their victim/victimer ethos to the next generation like the plague.

You should only become a teacher if you have no other choices. If you must be at the scene where learning takes place—if that is the most real place in the world for you. There is no other reason to be a teacher. If ideas are not your passion, do something else. Try acting.

• Fourteen-year-olds are the most interesting people alive—the most honest, the most spiritual, the most idealistic, and the most skeptical.

• Beware of teaching at the university. They have many accomplished minds there, and once a mind is accomplished, it is finished.

• Teaching at a college is nothing like teaching the ninth grade. At a college, the years and the courses fade in and out of each other like so many scattered birds. But ninth graders stay in your mind and memory forever—indelibly.

• The difficulty of teaching does not stem from its complexity, but rather from the fact that it demands total surrender and total vigilance. It is not an intellectual activity so much as a moral and a perceptual one. That is why some of the best teachers are not necessarily the best thinkers. Their genius resides in their capacity to invest so much significant attention to their subjects that the outer world just disappears. They possess a capacity to give their lessons such intellectual urgency that the conventional life loses all its appeal, and students enter into the bliss of pure philosophical absorption. Like a classic work, great teachers fascinate, not by their glamour or flash, but by their intensity, by their focus, and by the perennial worth of their ideas and themes.

• Genius does what it must; talent does what it can. Genius generates imperatives; talent avoids errors. Genius learns from its mistakes to make adjustments to accomplish its own sublime ends; talent learns from its mistakes how to trim its wings to deflect criticism.

• I am bourgeois to the core and parochial beyond belief, and yet I am drawn to great art and scholarship as my anti-type, my shadow, the voice of distinction I never possessed. I don't think of myself as a teacher so much as an impersonator of profundities, inhabiting the wisdom of texts with the naked confidence that the value of the genius I espouse transcends the particular fraud that I am the one espousing it. And it doesn't matter that nobody seems to be listening to me. Those who listen that I don't know about are enough to keep me going, keep me living on the wing of borrowed metaphors.

Selected Readings

The Book of Proverbs. See especially Chapters 1–9. "More than all else, keep watch over your heart, since here are the wellsprings of life."

Plato, dialogues, especially the *Phaedrus.* In this mystic epistemology, Socrates points out the differences between the rhetoric whose aim is to deceive and the true rhetoric founded upon truth and logic. Contains the famous image of the soul as a charioteer driving two horses—one the divine will, the other irrational willfulness.

Lao Tzu, *Tao Te Ching*, Stephen Mitchell's translation. "Free from desire, you realize the mystery. Caught in desire, you see only the manifestations."

Aristotle, *Nichomachean Ethics.* Brings Plato down to cases with his doctrine of the Golden Mean. Virtue is an art, not a science; a practice, not a procedure. So is teaching.

Matthew 13. Jesus' famous discourse on parables. "I will speak to you in parables and expound things hidden since the foundation of the world."

Longinus, *On the Sublime.* This is a treatise on how to produce ecstasy through language. "We must nurture our souls to all that is great, and make them, as it were, teem with noble endowment."

Marcus Aurelius, *Meditations.* Stoic admonitions designed to calm and focus even the most stressed emperor—or teacher!

John Baptist De La Salle, *Meditations for the Time of Retreat.* Moving reflections upon the art of teaching as spiritual witness and struggle for justice. "You should learn to recognize Jesus beneath the rags of the poor children whom you have to teach."

William Wordsworth, *Preface to the Lyrical Ballads.* "For a multitude of causes, unknown to former times, are now acting with a combined force to blunt the discriminating powers of the mind, and unfitting it for all voluntary exertion, to reduce it to a state of savage torpor."

Ralph Waldo Emerson, "The American Scholar" and "The Divinity School Address." "A more secret, sweet and overpowering beauty appears to man when his heart and mind open to the sentiment of virtue. Then he is instructed in what is above him. He learns that his being is without bound; that to the good, the perfect, he is born, low as he now lies in evil and weakness."

Henry David Thoreau, *Walden*. There is, perhaps, no greater education than intimate contact with an original and free mind.

Matthew Arnold, *Culture and Anarchy*. "We, indeed, pretend to educate no one, for we are still engaged in trying to clear and educate ourselves. But we are sure that the endeavor to reach, through culture, the firm intelligible law of things—we are sure that the detaching of ourselves from our stock notions and habits—that a more free play of consciousness, an increased desire for sweetness and light, and all the bent which we call Hellenizing, is the master-impulse even now of the life of our nation and of humanity."

Friedrich Nietzsche, *Schopenhauer as Educator*. In this slim volume, the young Nietzsche examines one of his teachers according to his famous dictum, "I judge a philosopher by whether or not he is able to serve as an example."

Gustav Janouch, *Conversations with Kafka*. A rare glimpse of Franz Kafka as educator and friend, seen through the eyes of an admiring student. Filled with anecdotes, lessons, and conversations that challenge the conventional modernist view of the writer and reveal a sublime vision behind the dark, skeptical, probing imagination.

Martin Buber, *Tales of the Hasidim*. Contains hundreds of specific accounts of the sublime pedagogy in action. See also his essays "Education" and "The Education of Character" in *Between Man and Man*. "In spite of all similarities, every living situation has, like a newborn child, a new face that has never been before and that will never come again. It demands of you a reaction which cannot be prepared beforehand. It demands nothing of what is past. It demands presence, responsibility; it demands you."

Rainer Rilke, *Letters to a Young Poet*. The insights Rilke provides into the uses of solitude for self-creation are lessons from which any young teacher can take solace. See also the *Dunio Elegies*. "You should not let yourself be confused in your solitude by the fact that there is something in you that wants to break out of it. . . . People have (with the help of conventions) oriented all their solutions toward the easy and toward the easiest side of easy; but it is clear that we must hold to what is difficult."

Herman Hesse, *Journey to the East*. All serious teachers are on "the journey to the East." In this novel, Hesse explores the dynamics of this sacred, collective, largely hidden, spiritual quest. See also *The Glass Bead Game*, perhaps his most profound novel of education.

Warner Jaeger, *Paideia: The Ideals of Greek Culture*. Master overview of the spirituality of classical education. Published 1939–1944 as a witness against fascist and Bolshevik assaults upon Western humanism.

Simone Weil, "Reflections on the Right Use of School Studies with a View to the Love of God." "In every school exercise there is a special way of waiting upon truth, setting our hearts upon it, yet not allowing ourselves to go out in search of it." This essay explores those ways.

Aldous Huxley, *The Perennial Philosophy*. "An attempt to present the Highest Common Factor of all theologies by assembling passages from the writings of those saints and prophets who have approached a direct spiritual knowledge of the Divine, and who have recorded not only the method of that approach but also the clarity and tranquillity of soul they derived from it."

Dietrich Bonhoffer, *Letters and Papers from Prison*. See especially "Thoughts on the Day of the Baptism of Dietrich Wilhelm Rudiger Bethge" and "After Ten Years." "We have to learn that personal suffering is a more effective key, a more rewarding principle for exploring the world in thought and action than personal good fortune."

Jean Leclercq, *The Love of Learning and the Desire for God*. This classic study of monastic culture and spirituality does just what its title suggests: it links the love of learning to the desire for God.

Nikos Kazantzakis, *Report to Greco*. Account of Kazantzakis's education as an artist and seeker; emphasizes the role in his life played by his teachers: Christ, Buddha, Lenin, Zorba, Odysseus, and El Greco. A dramatic intellectual odyssey. "Three kinds of souls, three prayers: 1) I am a bow in your hands, Lord. Draw me, lest I rot. 2) Do not overdraw me, Lord. I shall break. 3) Overdraw me Lord, and who cares if I break!"

D. T. Suzuki, *The Training of the Zen Buddhist Monk*. This work by one of the most important religious figures of the century reveals the Zen version of the pedagogy of the sublime. See also his *Manual of Zen Buddhism* and *The Awakening of Zen*.

Thomas Merton, *No Man Is an Island*. This book is a frontal assault upon self-delusion and complacency. A fundamental primer for the art of self-reflection. See also *Conjectures of a Guilty Bystander* and *Vow of Conversation*, where Merton's contemplative understanding is brought to bear upon social problems. "In order to find God in ourselves, we must stop looking at ourselves in the mirror of our own futility, and be content to be in Him, to do whatever He wills, according to our limitations, judging our acts not in the light of our own illusions, but in the light of His reality which is all around us in the things and people we live with."

James Baldwin, "A Talk to Teachers." Examines one of the paradoxes of education: that precisely at the point when students begin to develop a conscience, many of them find themselves at war with their society.

J. Krishnamurti, *Think on These Things.* "The mind, with its cunning arguments, is not everything. There is something vast and immeasurable beyond the mind, a loveliness which the mind cannot understand. In that immensity there is an ecstasy, a glory; and the living in that, the experiencing of that is the way of education."

Elie Wiesel, *Somewhere a Master.* Powerful descriptions of learning and teaching as sacred activities. Emphasizes the mysterious, winding paths through which the soul *becomes.*

Jacob Needleman, *The Heart of Philosophy.* See Part Two, an account of Needleman's attempts to teach philosophy to high school students and the essay on Wittgenstein. Also contains a description of Needleman's own existential awakening *at age fourteen.*

Jonathan Kozol, *The Night Is Long and I Am Far from Home.* A powerful, ethical critique of contemporary education. Prophetic and moving. "I think the reverence that we feel for men and women who have been true teachers, and the way *that* love can change our lives, our vision, our perception of all things we know, and open up new areas of freedom and imagination we have never felt . . . this is, in the long run, what education is, and nothing else but this."

Index

cultural values," 1; versus
friend, 165; versus parent, 145;
way of the, 33, 147
teacher's honeymoon, 11
teachers: the best, 161; home life
of, 48–51, 165; moods of, 66,
67; professionalism of, 87, 141,
151, 160; survival of, 19,
143–44; with weak egos, 167
teaching: as "attempting the
impossible," 69; defined, 27,
143, 154; difficult material,
154; difficulty of, 168; English
composition, 81–90; as
"existential art," 128, 148–49,
152, 154; as a "game," 33; as a
"job," 1, 2, 20–21; literature,
111–23, 131–41; *Martian
Chronicles*, 116–18; *Night*,
118–21; ninth grade, defined,
35; as a "performance in
language," 159; as "prayer," 69;
sex education, 105–10;
Siddhartha, 115–16; social
justice, 91–103; social science,
71–79; at the university,
129–39, 168; as a "way to
learn," 31–34
Teaching Credential Candidates,
131
tests, 160
textbooks, 73, 152, 155

theology, 97
third world missionaries, 62
Tolstoy, Leo, 70, 154, 161
"Torso of Apollo," 162
tradition, 163
Turlock, California, 72

U.S. Marine Corps, 12
University of Chicago, 139
utopia, 72, 114

Venus of Wallendorf, 75
Vietnam veterans, 133
The Village People, 60
violence, 16–19, 102, 114
Virgil, 28
Virgin Mary, 55, 60

warrior *geist*, 35, 60
Wiesel, Elie, 118–21, 143–44
Wittgenstein, Ludwig, 86
Woolf, Virginia, 156
Wordsworth, William, 136
world bank, 94
World War II, 54
writing, 81–90, 111

Yeats, William Butler, 158
youth, 3–4, 28, 34, 107

Zapruder film, 99, 103
Zen, 149

About the Author

ROBERT INCHAUSTI is Professor of English at California Polytechnic State University. His earlier work, *The Ignorant Perfection of Ordinary People*, examines the lives of six visionaries: Mother Teresa, Lech Walesa, Martin Luther King, Gandhi, Aleksandr Solzhenitsyn, and Elie Wiesel.